NOTHING IS MORE REAL THAN NOTHING

Daniel James is an author and journalist from Newcastle upon Tyne in the UK. A journalist for national newspapers and magazines for over a decade, James was a finalist for young UK news writer of the year before he became an author. *The Unauthorised Biography of Ezra Maas* is his debut novel.

'… a maze of allusion and illusion. The ultimate postmodern noir novel (with femme fatales and body in a Hollywood pool)? It's left for the reader to decide. An ambitious, challenging, and beautifully-designed book.' – *The Times*

'The book leaves all possibilities open. Playful and witty… It forever asks questions and rarely makes the mistake of answering them.' – *The Guardian*

'An engaging myth, constantly being examined and questioned… a discussion of art, semiotics, philosophy, fake news, writing as reality, red herrings, cryptic clues, musings on the nature of existence… a noir-ish nightmare. Relax and enjoy the ride.' – *NB Magazine*

'The whole noir-ish tale is pulled down several rabbit holes and viewed through multiple halls of mirrors and comes over like a literary equivalent of Orson Welles' *F for Fake*, which is a very good thing.' – *The Crack*

'Closing the book… You breathe a sigh of relief, thankful that you've made it back to reality. But in the next blink of the eye, you realise that the world you've returned to is ever so slightly different from the one you left.' – *Subscript.it*

'Piecing together the legacy of Ezra Maas means piecing together the book, tracing the ghosts behind the lines.' – *Nothing In The Rule Book*

The following collection was completed without the authorisation of the Maas Foundation. Enquiries about Ezra Maas should be directed to: ezramaas.com

Nothing Is More Real Than Nothing

~~Daniel James~~

Valley Press

First published in 2022 by Valley Press
Woodend, The Crescent, Scarborough, YO11 2PW
www.valleypressuk.com

ISBN 978-1-915606-00-6
Cat. no. VP0201

Cover photograph by Envela Castel.
Cover and text design by Peter Barnfather.

With thanks to Mike Corrao.

Printed and bound in Great Britain by
Imprint Digital, Upton Pyne, Exeter.

Contents

Introduction:
A Game of Doubles

Anonymous

Daniel James is dead.[1] Or least he used to be. I'm not sure what to believe anymore.

And Maas Lives.

If there was ever any doubt about the latter, it was extinguished in 2022 with the release of *The Unauthorised Biography of Ezra Maas* special edition from the book's new publisher, Valley Press.

With this edition, Maas has truly returned to the world.

Regardless of what has gone before, this year, now and forever… Maas Lives. And that knowledge fills me with a growing dread, and no small amount of guilt for the part I have played.

But I'm getting ahead of myself. I was approached[2] to write an introduction to this collection – the first critical work dedicated to analysing and exploring *The Unauthorised*

---

1. In an unsettling development, this was intimated by one online reviewer who apparently confused Newcastle novelist Daniel James with American author Daniel Lewis James, who published under a pseudonym and was known for keeping his identity a secret. Daniel died in 1988.

Biography of Ezra Maas by Daniel James – and that is what I will attempt to do, without further digressions or interruptions, or at least, with as few as possible.

This is a landmark moment after all. This collection, the first of its kind, brings together the work of international academics and scholars, authors and artists, critics, and members of the extended Maas community. There are essays, fragments, writings, and artefacts, from Dr Helen Gorrill, Maureen Hosay, Associate Professor Michael Jeffries, Dr. Daniel Barnes-Bineid, Hanna ten Doornkaat, John Palmer, Magdalena Harper, Marc Nash, Matthew Cook, Meaghan Ralph, Nick Reeves, Ian Roden, Ted Curtis, Amy Lord, and PM Buchan, among others. The wide-ranging topics and themes explored by these contributors include authorship and identity, post-truth narratives, metaphysical detectives,

---

2. Approached might be the wrong word. Try as I might to distance myself from the book, it continues to haunt me, and I remain forever responsible for the consequences which continue to manifest from my decisions not to destroy it as Daniel instructed. Ultimately, I had little choice but to participate despite my attempts to leave the world of the book behind. The Maas Foundation's ongoing attempts to erase my friend's work from existence forced my hand, and parallel to this, I was increasingly disturbed by certain developments in my absence, namely reports of someone, a double, an actor – perhaps hired by my friend, perhaps not – claiming to be the real Daniel James. Knowing this not to be true, I had to establish the truth behind this doppelganger, behind this 'reflection of a reflection of a reflection'.

intertextuality, the value of art, celebrity culture, Maas's social media presence, and gender equality. Like the biography before it, this collection was published without authorisation or involvement from The Maas Foundation. Nevertheless, the publication marks an important year for fans of the enigmatic artist. *The Unauthorised Biography of Ezra Maas* special edition is undoubtedly the definitive version of the text, and its return saw the book receive the kind of national media coverage I hoped and believed it deserved.

It was a strange pleasure to see Ezra Maas's name in The Times this year, which described Daniel's biography as 'a maze of allusion and illusion… the ultimate postmodern noir novel… [and] an ambitious, challenging, and beautifully-designed book'.[3] Alongside this, the special edition of *The Unauthorised Biography* was also chosen for the permanent collection at The Library of Congress on Capitol Hill in the United States.[4] These parallel developments admittedly

---

[3.] thetimes.co.uk/article/the-best-new-crime-fiction-for-may-2022-wgcxhmop7

[4.] The Library of Congress on Capitol Hill, Washington DC, is the national library of the United States and the largest collection of books, recordings, photographs, maps, and manuscripts in the world. *The Unauthorised Biography of Ezra Maas* (Special Edition) can be found in the Jefferson Building and Adams Building reading rooms. Other notable documents in The Library of Congress include the rough draft of the Declaration of Independence and a Gutenberg Bible (originating from the Saint Blaise Abbey in the Black Forest) – one of only three perfect vellum copies known to exist.

felt like a vindication of my decision to betray my friend's wishes and the instructions he left for his work to be destroyed when he disappeared. It was a decision I made not to restore the name and status of Maas himself, but to ensure Daniel's work lives on and continues to reach new readers.[5] It has, without doubt, succeeded in doing just that, and on an international scale. A new generation of knowledgeable and well-read international readers, particularly in the US and Australia, have discovered and championed the book. Ben Lindner at Beyond the Zero[6] and Seth Corwin at W.A.S.T.E Mailing List[7] in particular must be commended for going above and beyond to recommend the book to their followers. As with its original release, The Maas biography has also continued to find fans amongst authors, artists, and academics, as well as with readers. Novelists such as Booker

------

[5.] The book's cult following has continued to grow over the years since the first edition was released, attracting new readers and reviewers from around the world, despite only having been published in the UK to date. Its status owes much to the readers who have championed the book, on and offline, and while I have kept away from the coverage of the book since leaving the UK, I have been made aware of the efforts of a number of readers and I would like to say thank you. While there are too many to name, I have tried to acknowledge as many readers and reviewers as possible on Pg. 253.

[6.] An international and highly recommended podcast discussing the very best books with knowledgeable readers, contemporary authors, and book critics. You'll find the BTZ podcast here: anchor.fm/beyondzero

Prize shortlisted author Graeme Macrae Burnet, Eisner-Award winner Bryan Talbot, Orwell Prize shortlisted author Glen James Brown, Desmond Elliott Prize winner Derek Owusu, BBC National Short Story finalist Richard Smyth, John Newsham, Olga Wojtas, Alison Baillie, Lucie Brownlee, Amy Lord, Ted Curtis, Philip Freedenberg, and many others, have supported the book. This year has also seen the first Ezra Maas art exhibition for more than three decades at a gallery in London, a resurgence in the infamous 'Maas Lives' graffiti tags found in cities as widespread as New York and Paris, the emergence of unsettling, viral videos with numeric codes online, the republication of Maas's Wikipedia entry after a number of years offline, renewed activity on the Maas Foundation website[8] and social media channels,[9] new connections[10] and hidden messages discovered in the changes between editions,[11] the reappearance of a stranger with Daniel's face, and even fans of the book bearing tattoos inspired by lines from *The Unauthorised Biography*.

[7.] With a focus on long form analysis rather than reviews, and an interest in fiction that is either lauded or maligned for complexity, ambiguity, and impenetrability, Seth Corwin's W.A.S.T.E Mailing List is another highly recommended space for literary discussion. Find W.A.S.T.E on Instagram: @wastemailinglist or subscribe to his YouTube channel for more.

[8.] ezramaas.com

[9.] Primarily Twitter (@MaasFoundation) where they have been active since 2012.

10. 'I've put in so many enigmas and puzzles that it will keep the professors busy for centuries arguing over what I meant, and that's the only way of insuring one's immortality.' – James Joyce. Maas connections continue to be discovered within the text years after the book's initial release as readers find new details hiding in plain sight within the book's many layers. Respected book reviewer Jonathan Pool should be noted for having dedicated almost an entire review to a selection of these diverse references – intertextual, cultural, philosophical, scientific, and more – many of which are found in the book's 500+ footnotes. Although his review is now several years old, Mr Pool has continued to find new connections in the book while revisiting the text. 'Whether intended or not, [the references I have found] are a great example of how the book, in the hands of readers, will reveal connections that even the original author might not have knowingly anticipated.' All of which lends further credence to a recent description of the book from reader Iain Smith as: 'Existential noir for "apopheniacs" (a description virtually served on a platter by the book itself). A "poioumenonic" page turner of nested narratives. It's a wrong footing, paranoiac ride, a proper head trip, where it can seem the book has a consciousness of its own.' Apophenia, of course, being the tendency to perceive meaningful connections between unrelated things. And yet, as William Burroughs reminds us, 'A paranoid is someone who knows a little of what's going on. A psychotic is someone who has just found out what's going on.'

It was my intention to begin this introduction, which has already deviated far from its remit, with an updated history of James' controversial biography, from 2012 to 2022 – it seemed a fitting place to do so given this collection's subject matter. While the history of the biography is best told within the book itself, what happened after its publication is almost as fascinating.

---

11. Shortly after the publication of the new special edition from Valley Press, reader and reviewer Paul Fulcher was the first to notice a deliberate change, a missing footnote/superscript, that may or may not signal a hidden message within the text. Another reader, Jeff Falzone, has highlighted a particular intertextual connection between the Maas biography and the work of the reclusive author Evan Dara, as well as a potential pattern within the punctuation. Other 'Maas observations' include the claim that the artworks in the new edition, when put under a blacklight, reveal an alpha-numeric code, potentially coordinates to a geo-cache location, where an unredacted version of the original manuscript has been hidden. Naturally, I cannot confirm or deny the latter, except to say that Daniel's original manuscript does exist in a damaged and incomplete state. However, I will never reveal its location.

However, I was quickly to discover that a respected literary reviewer,[12] and patron of the Republic of Consciousness Foundation,[13] had already published such an account. Rather than write over his work and create yet another palimpsest, I have decided to include a section of his 'troubled history' of *The Unauthorised Biography* here within this introduction.[14]

[12.] The aforementioned reviewer Paul Fulcher.

[13.] Founded in 2017, the Republic of Consciousness Prize exists to: 'To advance for the public benefit literary fiction of the highest merit from small presses in the UK and Ireland through a range of reading, speaking and event initiatives, and by providing grants and assistance to practitioners and producers of literary fiction.'

[14.] There is, of course, a pre-history to *The Unauthorised Biography* that precedes, and runs parallel, even to this account of the book's publication, dating back to independent arts magazine (*The Bleed*) which was distributed for free at venues in and around Newcastle with help from Trevor Pill, Andrew Mitchell, Dean Forbes, Peter Whitfield, Sam Molloy, and others.

With the author's permission, here is an extended extract:

- *You will only know I have succeeded if you do not know who Ezra Maas is, if the name means nothing to you. If he lives now, it is only in the pages of this book.*

A brilliant new special edition of one of the most important books of the last decade was published in May 2022. *The Unauthorised Biography of Ezra Maas* has had a troubled history, however.

Ezra Maas, 'the romantic artist, the withdrawn recluse, the violent, temperamental genius, the charismatic cult leader, the counterculture icon, the serial womaniser, the drug addict, the experimenter, the intense loner, the passionate collaborator, the painter, the poet, the madman,' was officially registered missing by the shadowy Maas Foundation in 2005 after a brilliant, but increasingly mysterious career. In the following years, his works were bought up, removed from public display, and newspaper stories about him suppressed. It was almost as if he had never existed.

In 2011, journalist and author Daniel James received a 3am phone call from the representative of a mysterious, and never identified, third party, offering him a huge sum simply to write the 'unauthorised biography' of Ezra Maas, and to find the truth behind both his origins and disappearance. His investigations took him around the world, and placed the lives of himself, and others, at risk.

Then in May 2012, when his book was about to be launched, the Maas foundation scheduled a press conference, claiming Maas was alive and well and ready to unveil his master work. The book was dropped by James's original mainstream publisher (under pressure from the Maas Foundation?), William Wilson & Co.[15]

And in 2013, James himself went missing.

The evidence suggests James tried to destroy his research and his writing. But an anonymous former close companion of James who prefers to remain anonymous, the Brod to James' Kafka, has reassembled what survives, and published it under Daniel James's name.

[15.] The book's original publisher, William Wilson & Co, referred to in the review above and whose name interestingly was inspired by the famous Edgar Allan Poe's story of doubles, were one of the UK's larger independent publishers, until 2012 – the very same year that Daniel's biography was first 'shelved' – when the publisher, its staff, and its entire catalogue, were purchased by one of the world's biggest publishing houses. Although we contacted this international mainstream publisher for a comment about the timing of their purchase in relation to the decision to shut down Daniel's book, as well as rumours of the Maas Foundation's involvement in both, they not only refused to contribute to this introduction, but also threatened legal action if they were named.

Shunned by the large conglomerates, (again as a result of pressure from the Maas Foundation?) the book was picked up and published in a crowdfunded campaign by a small independent press in November 2018.

Here are extracts from my original review:

The book interweaves four separate sections:

— what remains of James's official biography, at times rather hagiographic, as much of what remains of Maas's history has been controlled by the Foundation.

— oral accounts of those who knew him (a filmed example from Bryan Talbot, father of the UK graphic novel, is available on YouTube). Notably the picture of Maas that emerges from these different accounts — even the descriptions of his physical appearance — are highly contradictory: was he one man or many?

— Daniel James's own account of his investigations into Ezra Maas, written in a self-aware style that combines existential and metaphysical noir, auto-fiction, and new journalism.

— copious footnotes from the anonymous narrator (the anonymity presumably as he or she wishes to avoid the fate of James and Maas), both clarifying various references but also adding his own commentary on the story and the disappearance of James. But these footnotes, while answering many questions, raise a key one of their own — who exactly is the mysterious narrator — James himself, Ezra Maas or one of his representatives, or someone else?

It is a fascinating mix. Indeed, it is more than just a book, it's a work of conceptual art.

The book was initially hailed by readers as a work of genius, and shortlisted for the *Guardian*'s Not The Booker Prize, decided by readers not critics, a runaway winner of the public vote.[16] But – it isn't hard to guess whose hands were at work – the judges of the prize overruled the public vote, the book's then publisher seemed to mysteriously lose interest in promoting the book, which one suspects wasn't entered for the Booker Prize itself, and despite impressive sales, it went out of print.

In May 2022, Valley Press reissued *The Unauthorised Biography of Ezra Maas* in a brilliant new edition, with superb production quality that does the work justice. Wonderfully, given what many feared had become of him, Daniel James himself has apparently resurfaced.

---

[16] Mr Fulcher's twin brother, Graham, also a respected reviewer, had an interesting insight into this controversy having previously served as a judge on the NTB awards (although not that particular year). He said: 'The process in itself was mysterious. The book was the runaway winner of the public vote only to be overturned in the judges meeting – a meeting which in every other year was broadcast live (in fact complete transparency of the judging process is the raison d'être of the awards) but which mysteriously that year was neither broadcast nor even recorded due to "gremlins".'

And the new edition contains some explicit additional information, but also some interesting secrets of its own.[17]

But be careful...

It is impossible to discount the possibility that some of what you are about to read may contain fiction.

You know that line 'the greatest trick the devil ever pulled was convincing the world he didn't exist'?

Well, I think Ezra Maas's greatest trick was convincing the world he did.

Some stories are more dangerous than others, and true stories are the most dangerous of all.

This book is dangerous.

You need to know that before you begin... ◆

[17.] For more on this, see some of Paul Fulcher's social media posts on the subject highlighted in 'Unauthorised Social Media' on Pg. 169 of this collection.

Thus ends the reviewer's updated review. An interesting detail, which admittedly sounds like it has been lifted from the pages of a book by Daniel James, is that the reviewer is a twin. His brother is also a respected online literary reviewer[18] and, just like his twin, he was another champion of *The Unauthorised Biography of Ezra Maas* on its release:

> *The Unauthorised Biography of Ezra Maas* is a multi-layered examination of identity and myth, and a magnificent hybrid of multiple literary forms that is never less than enthralling.

Despite the book's troubled and controversial history to date, and despite the inevitable speculation that the Maas Foundation played a role in this, I am relieved to say that the book survived the many attempts to discredit, censor, and silence it, and has continued to reach readers around the world. Even when it went temporarily out of print, I somehow knew it would return. It was as if the book itself – Daniel's words and Ezra's truth – had the power to force its own way back into existence. Over the last three years, slowly but surely, the biography's cult status has continued to grow and gain momentum, perhaps in part because of the very attempts to bury and burn it, helping to further establishing the book as a forbidden text.

The book's resurrection undoubtedly culminated[19] in the events of 2022. The visionary special edition of *The Unauthorised Biography of Ezra Maas* was published by Valley

---

18. The aforementioned Graham Fulcher.
19. 'Reached a critical mass?'

Press, with a double launch event in London and Newcastle, followed by the release of the very book you hold in your hands right now, *Nothing Is More Real Than Nothing*, with its title inspired by the words of Samuel Beckett.[20]

With the publication of this collection, and before it the definitive special edition of the book, both Maas himself, my friend Daniel, and his biography of the artist, have returned to the world, for better or worse. Perhaps one cannot live without the other? Where, I wonder, does that leave me in all of this? Little more than a ghost, I fear.

I must, of course, refrain from this kind of speculation and return to the matter at hand; concluding the introduction to this collection. While I played no part in its assembly, I still want to take this opportunity to thank those who made it happen – the contributors[21] for their brilliant and diverse writings on both the subject of Ezra Maas and Daniel's biography of the artist, the book's designer Peter Barnfather,[22] cover photographer Envela Castel,[23] and the publisher Valley Press.

---

20. The title is also a reference taken from my old friend's PhD thesis on Beckett's Trilogy of novels (*Molloy*, *Malone Dies*, and *The Unnamable*) – research, which coined the phrase 'The Literature of Psychosis', a term that more and more has come to refer to his own work.

21. For the full list of contributors, their bios, and for where to view more of their work, see Pg. 254–256.

22. A cover designer and publisher, Peter Barnfather's designs have been shortlisted by The Academy of British Cover Design. (peterbarnfather.com)

In my foreword to *The Unauthorised Biography*, written several years and, what feels like, many lifetimes ago, I warned those who would follow in my footsteps. I told you then, what I will tell you now; this book is dangerous. I say this with the knowledge that if you have come this far, if you are reading this, then you are already inside the many interconnected, Rhizomatic[24] passageways that make up the book,[25] trapped within its infinite reflections; you are part of it now.

> Every reader changes the story, bringing it to life
> and making it real, every reader plays their part,
> just as I have played mine.

There are no words left and there is nothing that I could say that would save you now for there is no way out. And

---

[23.] French photographer Envela Castel has developed her own style based on cinematic and dramatic aestheticism. She is driven by art and the ancient world, which is why her personal projects tend to focus on History and ancient civilisations, taking her around the world and documenting the past and its consequences on our society today. For more go to. (envelacastel.com)

[24.] 'Maas of roots' – A rhizome is a concept in post-structuralism describing a nonlinear network that 'connects any point to any other point'. Deleuze and Guattari use the terms *rhizome* and *rhizomatic* (from Ancient Greek ῥίζωμα, rhízōma, 'mass of roots') to describe theory and research that allows for multiple, non-hierarchical entry and exit points in data representation and interpretation.

yet, words are all that I have left and all that I can offer you. We all have our parts to play as Daniel said, and perhaps there is some hope to be found in this, between the lines, within the nothingness, for in the end…

---

25. A labyrinth of interconnected passageways and infinite reflections – physical and psychological, print and digital, tangible and intangible. Or as Daniel wrote: 'An infinite sphere, whose centre is everywhere and whose circumference is nowhere.'

...nothing is more real than nothing.

DON'T

READ

THIS

BOOK

The Maas Polaroids

Associate Professor Michael J. Jeffries,

THE MAAS POLAROIDS

The history of the five MAAS POLAROIDS presents a cautionary example of the challenge to art historians intent on mapping Maas' time spent in the United States in the late 1970s.

The artefacts comprise five Polaroid SX70 photographs, taken in the late 1970s, coincident with Maas' return to New York between 1977–1980. The five were found in one of Andy Warhol's month boxes[26] wrapped in a tissue marked EM TO AW, an obvious play on Warhol's autobiography published a couple of years before (Warhol, 1975). At first glance the Polaroids appear to show celebrities, including Warhol, at Studio 54, the infamous New York Night club.[27] All five photographs have been damaged, intentionally cut to remove a portion of the image, the shape, size and position of the excision suggesting the removal of someone who would

---

[26.] Warhol kept much of his day-to-day detritus, boxing it up every month or so into a collection now called 'time capsules'. The boxes, over 600 of them, are held in the Warhol Museum in Pittsburgh (warhol.org/educators).

otherwise be central to the image, possibly Ezra Maas. Initial curatorial indexing attributed the Polaroids to Maas, the remnants of a night out with Warhol, whilst the damage was assumed to be the work of the Maas Foundation. However recent re-evaluation has been prompted by sophisticated anomalies with the Polaroid format, perhaps Maas himself, consciously subverting the apparently authentic instant capture of a Polaroid.

27. Studio 54 was a famed New York nightclub of the late 1970s. During its heyday between 1977 and 1979 the club was frequented by pop stars stars, politicians and celebrities, including Warhol, who would photograph the revellers.

All five photographs can be readily authenticated as late 1970s Polaroid. They are all SX70 format (the Warhol standard type). More specifically Polaroid films can be attributed using batch codes on the back of each photograph.[28] The five photographs all display month, year, and manufacture codes from a single packet from late 1977 or early 1978 and US factory sources. Warhol's own Polaroids often carry an embossed name stamp, sometimes a signature but these do not. Given that Warhol himself appears in two of the photos and is using his own Polaroid camera in one of them the pictures are unlikely to be Warhol's own. All five pictures show evidence of erased and scribbled over handwriting: the only readily legible example clearly reads CAPOTE and the picture is of Truman Capote. Analysis of the other images using methods such as infrared photography shows that the writing on these also just recorded the main celebrities in frame such as Salvador Dali or Henry Kissinger. Most intriguingly one of the photos features David Bowie, who had by this time moved to Berlin. Given that Mass also left the States and associated with Bowie in Berlin soon after the photograph suggests a remarkable and previously unrecorded contact.

[28.] Polaroid photographs have codes printed on the reverse proving remarkable detail of batch dates and manufacture (gawainweaver.com/images/uploads/file/Polaroid_ID.pdf). Chemical signatures can also be dated, Davies, N.A. 'Problems with the Dating of a Polaroid SX70 Photograph.' *Journal of Forensic Sciences*, vol. 38, 1993.

The Unauthorised Biography of Ezra Maas is a collage, with comic book speed, cuts and narrative; beautiful, incoherent and riddled with reinvented fragments.

Collage and comics play with the temporal and spatial, lurching between times and places. Collage resists structure (Dittmer, 2010). Similarly, the readers of Ezra Maas are allowed to make their own links in the chain, fill in the gaps, skip and ignore, not dictated to. Collage does not just toy with the format of novels or films, but also of academic disciplines. This is part of my delight with collage, photo-montage and comics, their alchemical, emergent properties, playing with the disciplines of geography and ecology in which I routinely research (Dittmer and Latham, 2015), and the biography. The superficially very familiar world of ponds and their wildlife is where I work; counting beetles and bugs, where they are and their comings and goings. However, counting beetles in one pond on one day is two dimensional. They might not be there tomorrow, nor were they the day before. Write up the science in a journal article and it is narrated and fixed. Statistical tests of significance give a precise mathematical measure but we soon forget that this is a quantification of uncertainty. My own papers titles try to remind the reader, for example 'elements of chance' or 'idiosyncratic' (Jeffries, 1989, 2003) I am drawn to that hinterland between the predictable, comfort laden 'balance of nature' and the uncertain, for example a water beetle could live in many ponds, able to fly around, but can only be in one at a time. The ecology of ponds is more a range of possibilities 'formless, non-sense and eventfulness' as Doel & Clarke (2007) wrote, but they were talking about collage, not ponds.

The initial attribution of the Maas Polaroids as the ephemeral memento of a night out at Studio 54 subsequently sliced and censored to deny Maas' participation has been subject to recent challenge. Whilst the physical objects are undoubtedly SX70 film from precisely appropriate dates and manufacture they all contain elements that do not accord with this narrative, All the photographs include objects that could not have been present in Studio 54, such as coloured vegetation from paleontological reconstructions (the film is black and white) and a zoomorph from a medieval beastiary or impossible interior alignments. Given that the pictures have all had sections cut out these could also have been removed so that their retention suggests they are supposed to be seen.

The instantaneous, inviolate nature of Polaroids has been a key part of their power, simultaneously undeniable and thoughtless. They carry the semiotic clout of untampered, but artists soon knew better (Indrisek, 2017). The possibility that these Polaroids have been manipulated suggests both a remarkable technical expertise and a critical intent very much in keeping with Maas.

CONCLUSION

The five Polaroids are unlikely to be the work of Warhol and more likely to be a satirical critique by Maas himself of the growing synergy between celebrity and art. Maas did want to be famous for just fifteen minutes.

Dittmer, J. 'Comic book visualities: a methodological manifesto on geography, montage and narration.' *Transactions of the Institute of British Geographers*, vol. 35, no. 2, 2010, pp. 222–236.

Dittmer, J. and A. Latham. 'The rut and the gutter: space and time in graphic narrative.' *Cultural Geographies*, vol. 22, no. 3, 2015, pp. 427–444.

Doel, M.A. and D.B. Clarke. 'After images.' *Environment and Planning D: Society and Space*, vol. 25, no. 5, 2007, pp. 890–910.

Indrisek, S. 'A brief history of Polaroids.' *Artsy*, 12 Jul. 2017, artsy.net/article/artsy-editorial-history-polaroids-art-ansel-adams-andy-warhol.

Jeffries, M.J. 'Measuring Talling's "element of chance in pond populations".' *Freshwater Biology*, vol. 20, no. 3, 1988, pp. 383–393.

Jeffries, M.J. 'Idiosyncratic relationships between pond invertebrates and environmental, temporal and patch-specific predictors of incidence.' *Ecography*, vol. 26, no. 3, 2003, pp. 311–324.

Warhol, A. *The Philosophy of Andy Warhol. From A to B & Back Again*. Harcourt, Brace, Jovanovich, 1975.

Drag Kings in the Artworld:
An essay on gender and success
[with a hypothesis on Ezra Maas]

Dr. Helen Gørrill

Everything really great and beautiful which we know
about, and everything which exists to charm our
astonished gaze, is the creation of men, the stronger
– and not of women, the fairer portions of mankind.
The temples of the Egyptians and Greeks, the gigantic
domes of the Middle Ages, the sculptures of the
Parthenon, the frescoes of the Vatican, and all the
other monuments which, century after century, have
been objects of pilgrimage to men of culture whose
souls are ever searching for the land of beauty – they
sprang from the masculine brain and were executed
by man's hard hand. (von Falke and Perkins, 1879)

I recently stumbled across an antiquarian bookshop in
the windswept streets of Scotland's national book capital,
Wigtown. Wandering from shop to shop, with over a quarter
of a million books to choose from, I struck gold.

After fifteen years of researching gender inequality in the
contemporary artworld, I had yet to find an historic tome
that specifically and explicitly explains why women should
not be artists – other than Honoré de Balzac's *Physiology of
Marriage* (1829) – which declares that wives must be denied

training and culture. In Dana Leslie's award-winning book *Performing Feminism: Self/Maintenance in Contemporary Art and Society* (2022), she states that 'even when learning a skill, for women the purpose was to remain mindlessly occupied as to not engage in any unwarranted, non-beneficial activities, such as art.' Leslie discusses a 1933 news article which reads, 'Wife of the Master Mural Painter Gleefully Dabbles in Works of Art' (Davies, 1933). The wife-artist whose work was not to be taken seriously, was the extraordinary painter Frida Kahlo. And as recently as 2017, Leslie tells us about the renowned contemporary artist Kate Miller, who was reduced to the headline, 'T. J. Miller's wife making a name for herself in New York' [since edited to actually include her first name] (Siegler, 2017). It is well known that women have historically 'belonged' to their husbands –my own mother always used to sign herself as belonging to a man – with her title as Mrs – followed by my father's first and second names (her own names invalidated). And it stands to reason that in historical society, women would largely have to do as they were told – or they would risk being executed for witchcraft, for stepping over the line into masculine boundaries – or become incarcerated for the manmade Victorian disease 'hysteria', the malady of the womb, where women would find themselves strapped to wooden benches to receive electrocution 'therapy' to enable them to return to the safe confines of traditional femininity. Today, women are still expected to comply and be submissive to society's demands. Many women still sacrifice their own careers to support their husbands and take care of their families.

My own book *Women Can't Paint* was written in response to the celebrated German artist, Georg Baselitz, who spends a lot of his time discussing with journalists why women should not be allowed to practice as artists in the 21ˢᵗ century (Clark, 2013 / Miller, 2015). In 'Sexism and ageism in visual art values' (Gørrill, 2020), the research evidences a new 'artworld hysteria', which stems from the Victorian version, and still affects women – artists – today. In our apparently gender-equal society, when [women] artists object to their gallerists' and dealers' oft-unreasonable demands, they are described as being 'mad' and subjected to accusations of mental health problems. There is no incarceration for the mythical disease today, and so the women are usually dropped by their galleries for making not unreasonable demands or suggestions – or as they see it – crossing over the boundaries of masculinity to assert themselves. Our predicament does not end there. When a man signs a work of art, it goes up in value, yet when a woman signs her work it goes down. There are few aesthetic differences in men's and women's painting, yet men's art is valued up to 90 per cent more. Museums are also complicit in this vicious cycle as they collect only tokenist female artwork which detracts from women artists' market value – a fact that is amplified, when we consider that mostly, our museums are publicly funded by taxpayers – and so it is also us, the general public, who are indirectly responsible for women artists' suppression.

I detest the term 'woman artist'. As I stated in *Women Can't Paint*, the feminine term 'actress' tends to be no longer used by the media, having been superceded by the word 'actor'. We no longer hear the terms 'lady solicitor' or 'woman accountant', and there is now a genderless noun 'firefighters' for those in that profession rather than 'fireman' or 'firewoman'. However, the term 'artist' [for men] and 'woman artist' [for women] has persisted. It has also led to a battle of the sexes, with 'critics' such as Alexander Adams, writing from the extreme right, who bizarrely claims that women have now taken over the world of art, to the detriment of men. Adams, who shuffled through a handful of press releases in his desperate attempt to find evidence to prove my Doctorate wrong. We have many male critics and art writers who tend not to cover the work of female artists. Male artists such as Adams, who haven't done as well as they thought they should have done through their own artwork's validation, turn to writing in order to wreath scorn upon anybody who might attempt to make something for themselves – very often, the brunt of men's scathing criticism – are [women] artists or [women] authors. Hence Georg Baselitz's *women simply cannot paint* allegations in 2013, 2015 and beyond; and Dana Leslie's discussion about the *wife* Frida Kahlo gleefully dabbling in paint together with T.J. Miller's *wife* attempting to make a name for herself in New York. And – in case you think you have stumbled into a historic argument – this is the 21st century. Women are still denigrated, suppressed, rejected and ridiculed, for attempting to become more successful (read 'masculine').

Allow me to return to the draughty streets of Scotland and my antiquarian bookshop of choice. The book I found – possibly the best 'explanation' for why women should not be allowed to create art – smells vaguely of mushrooms and vanilla. It is called *Art in the House: Historical, Critical and Aesthetical Studies on the Decoration and Furnishing of the Dwelling*. Written in 1879 by Jacob Von Falke and Charles Perkins, I flick through and pause on Chapter X. 'Woman's Aesthetic Mission':

> It is true that history also records the names of women
> who have actively laboured in the wide domain of the

arts of design, such as Sabina von Steinbach, Margaret van Eyck, Elizabetta Sirani, Angelica Kaufmann, Rachel Ruysch, and many women of our own time whose names might be deservedly added to the list. But how small and limited is the field which they cultivated, how insignificant is their number as compared to that of the men who have worked in the same sphere of human activity, and how far in the background must we place their achievements, if we take into consideration grandeur of style, depth and breadth of conception, elevation and boldness of idea, exuberance of life, energy and vehemence of passion!

If we look over the whole broad field of art, we shall find that the hand of woman has laboured with success in all but a very narrow portion of it. Instinctively true to her nature, she has preferred the minute and charming, the delicate and amiable, the tender and graceful, and has cultivated it diligently, lovingly, patiently with talent and skill even, but yet in a humble style. On her own ground woman may compete for the prize with the hope of winning it, though, when we acknowledge that she is great in her speciality, we must perforce acknowledge add, that her speciality is small.

Thus far, Von Falke and Perkins have instructed us to understand that women's artwork will never be as good as men's, based on their biology, or to put it more crudely, because they were born without a penis. Of course, to Sigmund Freud, women are simply lesser or substandard men who have been born without penises. I even recall reading that Freud linked their lack of penis with women's enforced leisure needlework in the 19th and early 20th centuries. The famed father of psychoanalyis perceived that endlessly sliding a needle in and out of evenweave cloth, would help to soothe girls' and women's 'penis envy', and stop them from feeling deprived and envious because the needle was a suitable penis-substitute for a woman. Around the same time, Von Falke and Perkins proceed to educate us as to how we might understand woman's contribution to the arts, which is threefold; namely 'domestic needlework', 'house decoration', and 'self-maintenance'. Dana Leslie (2022) discusses 'self-maintenance' in her chapter 'Becoming a man-made woman: goodbye housework, hello beauty work', in relation to the extraordinary routines carried out by women today in their question for visual perfection. And in *Women Can't Paint*, I write about gendered sexism and ageism in visual art values, reporting on a conversation I had with the prominent feminist artist Margaret Harrison (b. 1940), who declared, 'but men are allowed to be old or ugly!' during a discussion about artists' visual appearances.

In the 1980s, the YBA generation promoted art as being young and part of popular culture. Former British prime minister Tony Blair also promoted such a culture which fell under the legacy of 'Cool Britannia' – a term evoking a national renaissance in arts and culture pioneered by Britpop bands, Young British Artists, [young] filmmakers and fashion designers. It is arguable that this focus on youth, coolness, sexuality and fame may have cast a shadow over older practitioners, which particularly affected women during the 1990s and beyond.

Tracey Emin is a YBA who slid easily into the role of young artist-as-celebrity, surrounding by an enticing aura of youth, sexuality and glamour. Perhaps this connection between youth, sexuality and success has been recognised by younger emerging female artist, along with the birth and boom of social media and endless beautified selfies. Talented painters and artists such as Sarah Maple (b. 1985) have been said to play on their relative youth as a method of self-promotion, and Maple's practice has arguably been reliant upon her being young and glamorous, with her self-defining as '*The* Young British Artist'. Indeed, in 'The Medium is the Market', Julian Stallabrass (2004) argues that the artworld has become contaminated by corporate mass media culture:

> An emphasis on the image of youth, the prevalence
> of work that reproduces well on magazine pages,
> and the rise of the celebrity artist, work that cosies
> up to commodity culture and the fashion industry
> and serves as accessible honey pots to sponsors.

Indeed, artwork presented at the London art Fair in 2018 for example, shows an emphasis on women's youth and such work that could present well on a magazine page – the rise of young social media influencers – as artists such as Claire Luxton whose supersized glossy beautified selfies may not have the same appeal to followers and prospective sponsors or collectors if she were photographing herself semi-clad or unbeautified in her fifties, sixties and beyond. In common with most selfies, Karina Jakubowicz (2018) argues that 'instead of a paintbrush, the artist now uses make-up, lighting, and digital enhancement in order to achieve a certain level of perfection that is far removed from the reality.' As I wrote in *Women Can't Paint*, there is no suggestion that a middle-aged or older (female) artist could contribute to or appeal to, the culture described above in this way. Indeed, during an interview with Artnet News (2014), Margaret Harrison complained that when she was awarded a major arts prize, 'nearly all the press, including the BBC, responded with the phrase, "Pensioner wins big prize!"' Margaret claimed that when older male artists had won this prize, their age had not even been discussed in the press. She perceived that the press intimated that it wasn't about the quality of the artwork but about the age and appearance of the woman artist. During my discussion with Margaret on art, age and beauty, it was clear she held very strong feelings from her experience of aging through her art career. Here's when she exclaimed, 'But men are allowed to be old or ugly!'

So where does this leave [women] artists who are not as young or glamorous as Sarah Maple, Claire Luxton et al.? If women are 'allowed' to succeed on the basis of their youth, glamour and sexuality – then what happens if they are old, perceived as ugly, and ageing?. I interviewed a prominent artist in New York who claimed that her gallerist had threatened to drop from his books when she had a baby in her forties, and when the press described her cruelly as a 'has-been', the gallerist started shunting her to the back of the room when the press photographers were around. He suggested plastic surgery, botox, fillers. The talented artist was eventually 'let go' to make way for a younger, more attractive female artist. In the visual arts (Gørrill, 2020), we assume that it is the artwork that is important, rather than the visual appearance of its creator. In the case of female artists, however, the focus tends to shift onto her physical appearance as I outline below in *Women Can't Paint: Gender, the Glass Ceiling, and Values in Contemporary Art*:

In the 2014 novel The Blazing World, author and cultural theorist Siri Hustvedt tackles the long-debated issue of artworld misogyny. The book – a work of fiction – concerns a repressed older female painter living in New York. Artist Harriet Burden has become so frustrated with her lack of artworld recognition that she persuades three male friends to show her work under their own names. Until that point, Burden is invisible: wife and middle-aged mother foremost, her occupation as artist viewed as trivial and inconsequential. She is in fact an ageing woman attempting to encroach the peripheries of a man's world, and it is apparent she will never make it past he boundaries of acceptance and validation: Burden has passed the fruitful promises of childbearing age and decorative youth that her artworld's men allow to encroach ujpon them. She is fading away and disintegrating into her husband's shadow and a world of obscurity.

Nicole Porter (2007) argues that 'older women face a unique type of discrimination based on the intersection of their sex and age.' Older women TV presenters Arlene Phillips, Miriam O'Reilly, Moira Stuart and Selina Scott have all lost their jobs and been replaced by younger models. Older male presenters such as Bruce Forsyth were still presenting until late in their eighties alongside younger, very attractive female counterparts. As one of my famous artist interviewees told me 'men are allowed to be visible and old, women are not.' In 'Newsreaders as eye candy,' Wolfe and Mitra (2012) argue that women in the public eye 'still face much greater pressure than men regarding their physical appearance and body image.' While Wolfe and Mitra's research examines the importance of a youthful physical appearance in the TV industries, the impact of physical attractiveness on women's social status and interactional power could easily be applied to the careers of well-known women in the artworld. It becomes apparent, then, that had Siri Hustvedt's fictional character Harriet Burden been born male, she would not have had to disguise herself through her manufactured [younger] masculine persona(s). We cannot help but sympathise with Burden. Perhaps you would do the same thing, if you were to be put in her position? Having a wealth of talent and having every door closed in your face, why not become incognito and mask as a male, if this meant you could succeed?

There are other notable examples of female visual artists remaining illusive and mysterious – most notably that of the graffiti art star Banksy, and potentially the illusive Ezra Maas. The recent Bloomberg article 'Why Banksy is (probably) a woman' (Capps, 2014) states, 'Since there's so much misdirection and jamming of societal norms with Banksy's work, as well as the oft-repeated claim no one notices Banksy, then it makes sense... No one can find Banksy, because they are looking for, or rather assuming, that Banksy is a man.'

According to *The Independent* (Sommerlad, 2019) journalist Craig Williams has suggested that Banksy 'is really a collective of artists associated with [the musicians] *Massive Attack* rather than one person, cross-referencing the sudden appearance of Banksy murals with the band's tour dates in a viral blog post of August 2016, finding a number of matches.' The British broadcaster Jeremy Vine, speculates that Banksy is probably female. Vine stated, 'For a while, I've suspected that Banksy may be a woman and I'm starting to think that she's deliberately leading us astray' (Green, 2020).

It is clear to see that if Banksy were female, and appeared in public as a woman, particularly in the masculine world of graffiti she would have had little chance of success. The masculinity of street art has curiously, recently been impacted upon through the adult website Pornhub, who have launched their own graffiti-art spray paint entitled 'Pornhub Orange' in attempts to mainstream their main activity of adult entertainment. In the promotion for their artist's paint, they feature well-known American graffiti artists – all male of course – with female porn models promoting the paint through writhing and titillating the viewer in front of the exhibited artwork where the male presides with his orange can of paint. Of course, this relates very much to the male-as-master, female-as-muse artworld.

Graffiti art is well known for its masculine-domination, and even more so for its rejection of the LGBTQ+ community, which several of my current trans students have found themselves struggling with. In her article 'Why have there been no great women [street] artists?' Vanessa Silvera (2020) examines the reasons for women's exclusion from wider conversations about street art. She states that in the domain of street art, there are additional obstacles for anybody who is not cis-male who tags – such as a lack of role models. Moreover, it is noted that tagging is largely an exterior artform, which surely harps back to the Victorian ideal of women with-in, men with-out – women were very much confined to the interiors both in their domestic lives and in the way they created artwork. And there are key links between ephemeral street artworks and digital limited artworks: Non-Fungible Tokens (NFTs) – graffiti artworks are now being painted to be destroyed, created not for the location but for the metaverse and for investment. By using genderless names, women might stand a chance of success in the dizzying, oft-confusing world of NFTs, where non-works, or images of paintings for example might sell for millions of dollars. As we see that a direct correlation between street art and NFTs exist, this is yet another very contemporary obstacle that women – non-binary artists – anyone who does not identify as male – need to leap over, in order to acquire artworld equality. Historic, modern or contemporary – art made by women is very often cast aside, simply due to the biology of its creator. There is no wonder, then, that artists such as Burden, Banksy, and Ezra Maas have chosen to remain incognito.

In *The Unauthorised Biography of Ezra Maas*, author Daniel James questions,

> [Was Ezra Maas] a collective of artists rather than
> a single person? Is this why Maas is never officially
> seen in public, does not give interviews, or allow
> photographs to be taken, and has never attended any
> of his exhibitions or launches? This theory would mean
> that Ezra Maas was the creation of [Helena Maas]
> and the Maas Foundation, rather than the other way
> around, and the so-called followers and assistants who
> make and sell his work are essentially all Ezra Maas.

But more likely, if my research on gender and value is anything to go by, Ezra Maas is – or was – more likely to be/have been a female artist, if not a female operating her own collective of male assistants. Similarly, the Canadian media artist Chris Healey has maintained for years that Banksy is actually a team of seven artists – led by a woman (Munro, 2014). The artist Hanna ten Doornkaat agrees on the Ezra Maas hypothesis: 'What if Ezra Maas is, or was, a female artist like the main protagonist in Siri Hustvedt's novel *The Blazing World*?' All the while, our female protagonists live incognito, masking as men and concealing their real identities, so they can earn enough money to continue to make their art.

It could be argued that our female Banksy, and Ezra Maas are 'drag kings' – female performance artists who dress in masculine drag. With the popularity of Ru Paul's *Drag Race*, we are more familiar with drag artists who identify as men, but present themselves in feminine ways as part of a performance. If Banksy and Maas are cis-gendered women, and their personas are male, their art practices are performative. As part of their performance, many drag queens and kings have a separate drag persona in addition to the self they live as every day. This persona will of course look different, but may also have a different name and ask to be referred to by different gender pronouns (NCTE, 2017). If Banksy and Maas are drag kings – like Siri Hustvedt's Harriet Burden – once in character, they are able to escape the confinements of female repression, sliding out of their gilded cages and into their male sex, their success soaring as a result of a necessary gendered shift.

Let me return to the windswept high street in Scotland's National Book Town. The second book I purchased was by Del La Grace Volcano and Jack Halberstam: the beautifully photographed *Drag King Book*. In this tome, Volcano and Halberstam (1999) question

> What is a drag king? Why have drag kings not been
> as numerous or as popular as their drag queen counter-
> parts in popular culture? Are drag kings lesbians?

The Drag King Book tells you everything you've wanted to know, and more, about the lives and performances of contemporary male impersonators.

Drag kings are simply – as Volcano and Halberstam state – male impersonators. If Burden, Banksy and Maas are masquerading as men in order to succeed – they are simply male impersonators. In *Bustle*, Megan deMaria writes,

> Wouldn't it be great if, in 2015, there was finally an end to gender discrimination and inequality? Can you imagine a world where young girls could go to school, choose their own career paths, and make names for themselves in this world? We've still got a while to go before reaching gender equality in America and abroad, but that hasn't stopped strong women (and men) from fighting the good fight. But what about women from back in the day who had trouble being heard for the sheer fact that they were women? Plenty of strong women in history pretended to be men because frankly there just weren't many options and they wanted to, well, get shit done.

DeMaria reminds us of course, that women posing as men is not a new concept, stating, 'even today, women have to be characterised as male to be taken seriously in their professional lives'. This is particularly the case for women who experience an uphill struggle in male-dominated industries. The artworld is particularly masculine – in 2014, the Tate allocated just 13% of their budget to acquiring work made by women artists, there are multiple blue-chip galleries who still refuse to represent our female creatives, and we have a 90% gender (art) value gap in fine art painting sales – the worst gender pay gap of any other industry at present (Gørrill, 2020).

The notion of women posing as men in order to succeed is something we have often seen in literature – in the 19th century Mary Ann Evans chose to publish her books, including *Middlemarch*, under the pen name George Eliot; the English novelist and author of *Jane Eyre* used the gender-neutral pen name Currer Bell; and the Brontës published under Ellis and Action Bell. Brontë later wrote that the women had deliberately chosen names that were 'positively masculine' because female writers were 'liable to be looked on with prejudice' (DeMaria, 2015). According to DeMaria, the female authors 'wanted their writing to be given its fair due by critics and readers – even if that meant writing under false names.'

And DeMaria writes, while it is of course great that male disguises help these women achieve their goals – let us hope that in the future – that women can be respected on their own merits. Let us hope that women will not have to live incognito with their real identities concealed. Let us hope that women will not have to pose as men to gain respect – and in the case of Ezra Maas, let us hope that she will not have to continue living as a man in order to achieve her deserved artworld validation.

Adams, A. 'True Feminism has Never Been Tried, Comrade.' *The Critic*, 5 Mar. 2020, thecritic.co.uk/true-feminism-has-never-been-tried-comrade.

Artnet News. 'We Asked 20 Women, "Is the Art World Biased?' Here's What They Said.' *Artnet News*, 16 Sep. 2014, news.artnet.com/art-world/we-asked-20-women-is-the-art-world-biased-heres-what-they-said-81162.

Capps, Kriston. 'Why Banksy Is (Probably) a Woman.' *Bloomberg UK*, 4 Nov. 2014, bloomberg.com/news/articles/2014-11-04/why-banksy-is-probably-a-woman.

Clark, Nick. 'What's the biggest problem with women artists? None of them can actually paint, says Georg Baselitz.' *The Independent*, 6 Feb. 2013, independent.co.uk/arts-entertainment/art/news/what-s-the-biggest-problem-with-women-artists-none-of-them-can-actually-paint-says-georg-baselitz-8484019.html.

Davies, F. 'Wife of the Master Mural Painter Gleefully Dabbles in Works of Art.' *The Detroit News*, 1933, openculture.com/2015/03/1933-article-on-frida-kahlo-wife-of-the-master-mural-painter-gleefully-dabbles-in-works-of-art.html [accessed 17 Dec. 2021].

de Balzac, Honoré. *Physiology of Marriage* (1829). West Margin Press, 2020.

deMaria, Meghan. '11 Badass Women In History Who Pretended To Be Men.' Bustle, 25 Sep. 2015, bustle.com/articles/112732-11-badass-women-in-history-who-pretended-to-be-men-because-gender-equality-back-then-was.

Gørrill, Helen. *Women Can't Paint: Gender, the Glass Ceiling and Values in Contemporary Art.* Bloomsbury, 2020.

Green, Simon. 'Banksy "could be a woman" as Jeremy Vine notices "clue" in new artwork post.' *The Daily Star*, 16 Apr. 2020, dailystar.co.uk/tv/banksy-could-woman-jeremy-vine-21877576.

Hustvedt, Siri. *The Blazing World.* Sceptre Books, 2014.

Jakubowicz, Karina. *An Analysis of Griselda Pollock's Vision and Difference: Feminism, Femininity and the Histories of Art.* The Macat Library, 2018.

James, Daniel. *The Unauthorised Biography of Ezra Maas.* Valley Press, 2022.

Leslie, Dana. *Performing Feminism Self/Maintenance: in Contemporary Art and Society.* Boom Publications Ltd, 2022.

Miller, M.H. 'Update: Georg Baselitz Still Thinks Women Can't Paint.' *ArtNet News*, 20 May 2015, artnews.com/art-news/news/update-georg-baselitz-still-thinks-women-cant-paint-4203.

Munro, Cait. 'Could Banksy Be a Woman?' *Artnet News*, 5 Nov. 2014, news.artnet.com/art-world/could-banksy-be-a-woman-156971.

NCTE (National Center for Transgender Education), 2017.

Porter, Nicole. 'Sex Plus Age Discrimination: Protecting Older Women Workers.' *Denver University Law Review*, vol. 81, 2007, p. 79.

Siegler, M. 'T. J. Miller's wife making a name for herself in New York.' *Page Six*, 24 Jun. 2017, pagesix.com/2017/06/24/tj-millers-wife-making-a-name-for-herself-in-new-york [accessed 17 Dec. 2021].

Silvera, Vanessa. 'Why Have There Been No Great Women [Street] Artists?' *Haute Magazine*, 11 Dec. 2020, hautemagazinestandrews.com/creative-culture/why-have-there-been-no-great-women-street-artists.

Sommerland, Joe. 'Who is Banksy? The suspects linked to the art world's biggest mystery.' *The Independent*, 5 Nov. 2019, independent.co.uk/arts-entertainment/art/features/banksy-who-is-artist-secret-likely-candidates-names-public-sothebys-auction-a8590041.html.

Stallabrass, Julian. *Art Incorporated: The Story of Contemporary Art*. Oxford University Press, 2004

Volcano, Del la Grace, and Jack Halberstam. *The Drag King Book*. Serpent's Tail Books, 1999.

von Falke, Jacob, and Charles C. Perkins. *Art In The House: Historical, Critical, And Aesthetical Studies On The Decoration And Furnishing Of The Dwelling*. L.Prang & Company, 1879.

Wolfe, Claire, and Barbara Mitre. 'Newsreaders as eye candy: the hidden agenda of public service broadcasting.' *Journalism Education*, vol. 1, no. 1, 2012, p. 92.

Playing detective:
the metaphysical detective story in
The Unauthorised Biography of Ezra Maas

Maureen Hosay

> It was a wrong number that started it, the telephone
> ringing three times in the dead of the night.
> – *City of Glass*

> It began with a phone call in the dead of the night.
> – *The Unauthorised Biography of Ezra Maas*

INTRODUCTION

The Unauthorised Biography of Ezra Maas sets the tone from the very first pages: 'The following manuscript was completed without the authorization of the Maas Foundation' (James unpag.). This initial *mise-en-abyme* (the manuscript is the subject of the novel) is one of the numerous metafictional features that it exhibits. More precisely, *The Unauthorised Biography* is inscribed in a long tradition of metaphysical detective stories, ranging from Poe's 'The Man of the Crowd' (1840) to Auster's *City of Glass* (1985), by way of Atwood's short story collection *Murder in the Dark* (1983) (Merivale and Sweeney). Even though the detective genre is 'highly formulaic' (Bernstein 150), it can 'be resuscitated to give urgent new voice to the postmodern condition' (Ibid.). Indeed, it has a strong metafictional potential, as the work of the detective and that of the writer, as well as that of the reader, mirror one another (Nealon 118). So what would the voice of the *Unauthorised Biography* say if one listened closely and carefully enough?

In this essay, I shall discuss Daniel James's use of the metaphysical detective genre in his *Unauthorised Biography* as both a self-reflexive and a self-sabotaging narrative device. Since the genre is characterized by, among other things, a lack of closure, the paratextual extensions of the novel will show how an open-ended narrative can expand outside the boundaries of the novel. Special focus will be devoted to the novel's multimedia extension to the world wide web as a concrete way to resist closure while maintaining and heightening the reader's engagement. By expanding the realm of the novel to the internet, James offers his readers a way to find out more about Ezra Maas, neither dead nor alive, but constantly treading an in-between, the realm of endless possibilities, his very own limbo.

Part One.
The metaphysical detective story

I. A DEFINITION

In order to better understand how a metaphysical detective story works, let us first consider the ways in which it subverts the traditional conventions of the detective genre. In *Le roman policier ou la modernité* (1992), Jacques Dubois mentions the following:

> (a) there is a crime and there is a criminal; b) a detective is commissioned to investigate; c) the detective is external to the drama; d) the detective investigates; e) the detective finds the criminal and brings him to justice; f) the detective is himself innocent (Dubois qtd. in Dechêne 18).

As for the metaphysical detective genre, it 'parodies or subverts traditional detective-story conventions [...] with the intention, or at least the effect, of asking questions about mysteries of being and knowing which transcend the mere machinations of the mystery plot' (Sweeney and Merivale 2). This results in conventions that 'work in opposition to [those] of the 'classical' genre' (Dechêne 30), namely:

> [T]he defeated sleuth [...]; the world, city, or text as labyrinth ; the purloined letter, embedded text, *mise en abyme*, textual constraint, or text as object ; [...] the missing person, the 'man of the crowd,' the double, and the lost, stolen, or exchanged identity ; and the absence, falseness, circularity, or self-defeating nature of any kind of closure to the investigation (Merivale and Sweeney 8).

From a theoretical perspective, the *Unauthorised Biography* ticks all the boxes: the story revolves around a journalist (Daniel James, thereafter James-character) wannabe sleuth, who attempts to write the (unauthorised) biography of a mysterious artist. The man in question, Ezra Maas, is foregrounded by his absence throughout the novel. In spite of the abundance of information shared about him in the novel, Maas remains as elusive as ever, from his background to his physical appearance, the readers leave the novel still wondering whether they know anything about the man at all. James-character's investigation ends up turning into a metaphysical and metafictional open-ended delirium, which circles back to the very beginning of the first chapter.

2. SUBVERSION OF LITERARY GENRES

The link between the role of writer and that of detective is established quite early on in the novel. Anonymous[29] states: 'Daniel was an expert in noir fiction and saw the role of biographer as a kind of literary detective' (James 43). As a case in point, Anonymous discusses how James presents his investigation: '[Daniel] skips over much of th[e] research [about Maas] and instead chooses to portray this period of research as a kind of detective story [...]. He depicts himself throughout as a neo-noir literary detective' (Ibid.). This highlights James's fondness of the genre, as well as tendency to unreliability. Aside from being a metaphysical detective story, the novel can also be described as (1) a pseudo(auto) biography, and (2) a work of historiographical metafiction.

[29.] The unnamed individual who comments on James-character's manuscript in the footnotes.

(1) Pseudobiography

The fact that Daniel James is both the name of the author and that of the protagonist highlights the pseudobiographical nature of the novel, a 'major postmodernist grouping []' (Sweeney and Merivale 20) that Sweeney and Merivale suggests deserves further investigation. In that sub-genre, 'finding the "missing person" characteristically leads […] to discovering that we are him or her' (Ibid.). This discovery of the self through the missing person echoes the outcome of the metaphysical detective story. Stephen Bernstein argues that such works…

> …become more like works of literary criticism than fictional depictions of crime and detection. Hence, the metafictional intrusions of authorial figures in all three works: an exploding system of *Doppelgänger*[30] finally collapses into a number of closural scenes of reading, with reader-writer confrontations that manifest textual instability (Bernstein 135).

This statement largely applies to the *Unauthorised Biography*, in which James and Anonymous are authorial figures, with the latter also being the former's first reader. The result is the creation of 'a metafictional aesthetic which requires that characters double not only one another, but the author as

---

[30.] For more on the doppelgänger trope, see Magdalena Harper's essay 'Through the looking-glass: Ezra Maas, the Man in the Mirror'. This volume.

well' (Ibid.). James-writer, James-author, Ezra Maas, Daniel Maas (Ezra's brother), Anonymous, the mysterious writer 'Quinn', and James's unnamed email correspondent all end up 'collapse[ing] into one another through their own labyrinthine […] interrelationships and then, finally, into multiple of the author himself' (142). In the novel, the pseudobiographical genre fills two main functions:

> (a) It seeks to fragment and disseminate the author's identity, while at the same time trying to reconcile them. As such, the novel exhibits the tendency to self-parody that Salwa Karoui-Elounelli associates with the metafictional novel. Its goal is to 'retrieve the myth of authorial control, albeit in terms of self-derision' (Karoui-Elounelli 77):

> [T]he writer re-emerges as an interpreter of his own work, whose (re-)reading is informed by the mode of self-irony and displays an awareness of the paradoxical fact that the authorial myth cannot be resurrected except in self-flaunting, self-defeating terms (Ibid.).

As far as the *Unauthorised Biography* is concerned, the re-emergence of the interpretative voice[31] is embodied by the figure of Anonymous. As mentioned previously, they re-lentlessly, almost in a self-sabotaging way, draw attention to James's use of the noir tropes and clichés, and points at the narrative devices used by James. For instance: 'In this, and

---

31. If re-emergence is taken literally, one could speculate that Anonymous is a later version of Daniel James.

other chapters, he foregrounds the signs and signifiers of noir in the visible exterior of the narrative, knowingly employing classic motifs to explore the "slippage" between reality and fantasy' (James 179). On several occasions, Anonymous also displays their encyclopedic knowledge.

> (b) Much like Auster in the *New-York Trilogy*, James 'peppers the [book] with autobiographical information' (Bernstein 142) in order to 'further blur[] the boundaries of characterization and fictiveness' (Ibid).

(2) Historiographical metafiction

This second function is tied to another important genre present in the novel. Historiographical metafiction can be defined as works that are 'intensely self-reflexive and yet paradoxically also lay claim to historical events and person-ages' (Hutcheon 5). In this case, the character of Maas is set against the backdrop of real places, events, and people (e.g. Warhol,[32] Bowie, etc.).

Conversely, other characters clearly foreground the realm of the fiction. Samuel Molloy, James's journalist friend, is a combination of Beckett's first name and one of his characters' last name.[33] Ariane, the French journalist, could be a reference to the mythical Ariadne, leading James through labyrinthine

---

[32.] If one looks carefully at pictures of Warhol's factory, one may spot a mysterious man wearing sunglasses.

[33.] From the trilogy *Molloy, Malone Dies*, The Unnamable.

(digital) trails. The mysterious author with whom James meets is referred to as 'Quinn,' which is a nod to writer-detective Daniel Quinn from Auster's *City of Glass*. The first name Ezra brings to mind the poet Ezra Pound, and the last name 'Maas' is a reference to Pynchon's Oedipa Maas in *The Crying of Lot 49*.

While the novel constantly treads the fine line between fiction and reality with the character of James, and the numerous references to real people, places, and events, it also fully acknowledges a highly literary and fictional nature by weaving the novel into a rich tapestry of intertextual references.

3. LITERARY DETECTIVE

The three different genres outlined in the previous sections highlight the playful nature of the novel and show that it offers readers the opportunity to investigate the mystery alongside the main protagonist. Delphine Letort aptly compares the deconstructive nature of metaphysical detective stories to a puzzle: 'la déconstruction est à l'évidence une aventure narrative qui affiche l'artificialité de la fiction, mais elle est aussi un jeu proposé au spectateur supposé reconstruire le récit, tel un puzzle dont on assemble des morceaux'[34] (Letort 203). The paradox of those works, as J.H. Dettmar

---

[34.] 'deconstruction is obviously a narrative adventure that showcases the artificial nature of fiction. It is also a game that the audience is invited to play to piece the plot back together, much like a puzzle' (my translation).

points out, is that they urge readers to read 'like a detective' the very 'tale which cautions against reading like a detective' (Dettmar qtd. in Merivale and Sweeney 2). In spite of the lack of closure that the readers eventually face, they have more ways to derive pleasure from playing detective. Indeed, the *Unauthorised Biography* offers several layers of mystery:

(1) The textual level: the use of the paratext, especially the footnotes, gives the book a labyrinthine and encyclopedic structure[35] that demands engagement on the part of the reader, and that requires a sense of direction, focus, and dedication in order to navigate through the numerous references and lengthy footnotes, let alone explore the paths that they suggest.

(2) The content level: The most mysterious parts of the plot revolve around Maas (and his alleged disappearance) and his Foundation, but also slowly but surely around James, his motive, his past, and his mysterious 'friend', Anonymous.

(3) The metaphysical level. At the end of the novel, the world within it collapses. The destruction of the narrative is not, however, a nihilist and hopeless move on the part of the author. As William Spanos argues "'de-composition or de-struction [of traditional plot form] is not [...] a purely negative one'" (Spanos qtd.

---

[35]. Like novels such as David Foster Wallace's *Infinite Jest*, Vladimir Nabokov's *Pale Fire*, Mark Z. Danielewski's *House of Leaves*, or Doug Dorst's *Ship of Theseus*.

in Nealon 120) as it can 'unleash plural possibilities insofar as such a postmodernist undermining' becomes the agency not just of despair but also and simultaneously of hope, that is of *freedom, the infinite possibility of free play*' (Ibid.).

In the next section, I will explore the ways in which James offers the readers such a possibility, thus fully exhibiting the playful side of the metaphysical detective story.

Part Two.
The paratext or 'the infinite possibility of free play'

I. THE PERITEXT AND THE EPITEXT

The encyclopedic and seemingly never-ending nature of the novel manifests through its use of the paratext, and more specifically its use of the footnotes. Initially theorized by Genette in *Seuils* (1987), the notion of paratext has been redefined a number of times (e.g. Graulund 2006; Skare 2019) and applied to a wide variety of fields (e.g. film studies, media studies, digital narrative, etc.). Whitin the scope if this paper, the working definition of the paratext will be the following: the paratext is 'the threshold of the text' which 'frames and at the same time constitutes the text' (Allen 103). The paratext can be divided into two complementary notions, that of the peritext, which includes 'elements such as titles, chapter titles, prefaces and notes' (Ibid.), and that of the epitext, which includes 'elements – such as interviews, publicity announcements, reviews by and addresses to critics, private letters and other authorial and editorial discussions – "outside" of the text in question' (Ibid.).

Like other experimental novels, the *Unauthorised Biography* plays on the ambivalent role of the peritext as being part of the fiction, but also as a way to mediate the fiction between author and readers. Oftentimes, the character expressing themselves in that space is a messenger, who foregrounds the fragile and volatile nature of the text. They often suggest that they came across the text by accident.[36] For instance, Anonymous states: 'I am not able to tell you my name, or how I came to be in possession of this manuscript. I know it may lead to speculation' (James 2). They also tell the readers that the manuscript belongs to them, which further highlights the inevitable nature of textual instability. By embodying textual transformations, instability, and mediation, Anonymous is a constant reminder that anything the readers read can be called into question, as far as both authorship and reliability are concerned. The passing down of the manuscript also plays on the permeable boundaries between

---

[36.] In *House of Leaves*, Johnny truant finds Zampanò's manuscript inside an trunk after the old man died; in The Ship of Theseus, the two protagonists, Jen and Eric, happen to be reading and annotating the same novel among the many books from the library; the plot from *La caverna de las ideas* goes from detective story to metaphysical detective story when the fictional translator decides to engage more fully with the book that he is translating and takes part in the narrative.

fiction and reality. The manuscript is the text, and exists within the text, the paratext, and the reader's reality. Not only that, but the *Unauthorised Biography* has also found its way into the world wide web.

2. MULTIMEDIA EXTENSION: A NEW WORLD (WIDE WEB) FULL OF POSSIBILITIES

Where other open-ended novels might leave readers wondering, James decides to keep them engaged and uses the space outside of the novel in a way that allows them to "'begin another quest in the new world full of possibilities'" (Russell qtd. in Nealon 120). James himself is very much aware of the crucial narrative role that digital media play:

> [T]he multimedia and mixed media extensions of the novel that gravitate around it […] [are] as much a part of the book as the text itself. The book is not simply the pages, the glue and the spine, nor the ink, its exact dimensions are uncertain and cannot be measured any more than we can ascertain the size of the universe. Perhaps, just like that, it is also changing and expanding (Holloway).

What James describes is what N. Katherine Hayles calls 'Work[s] as Assemblage' (Hayles 279), which…

> …can be thought of as clusters, […] [that] take the distinctive form of rhizomatic tendrils branching out from one another in patterns of fractal complexity. […] the WaA derives its energy from its ability to

mutate and transform as it grows and shrinks, converges and disperses according to the desires of the loosely formed collectives that create it. Moving fluidly among and across media, its components take forms distinctive to the media in which they flourish, so the specificities of media are essential to understanding its morphing configurations (Ibid.).

The qualities of the WaA are very much in keeping with those of the *Unauthorised Biography*: (a) its rhizomatic nature, which fittingly support the maze-like journey and maze-like reading experience; (b) its ever-changing nature, which strengthen the feeling that the mystery cannot ultimately be solved, yet compels readers to seek closure; (c) the 'loosely formed collectives' that disperse and multiply authorship, and which the readers can also be a part of;[37] (d) the specificities of the media used matter, insofar as they present the work with new formal constraints that can alter the narrative.

In the following section, I am going to discuss the different forms taken by the multimedia extension of the *Unauthorised Biography* and identify how the choice of medium affects the narrative. The multimedia extensions that I will discuss in this section are: The Maas Foundation Website and three related Youtube videos, the Ezra Maas Wikipedia page, Daniel James Writer's website and two related videos, and a picture of a 'Maas Lives' graffiti in Paris.

---

[37] This essay, and more broadly this collection, is one of the many expressions collaboration can take.

a. Foregrounding the (anti)-hero

Most information on Daniel James can be found in the 'about' section of his website:

> Daniel James is an author, journalist, and editor from Newcastle upon Tyne in the United Kingdom. His debut novel, *The Unauthorised Biography of Ezra Maas*, is out now. An arts and culture journalist for a decade, Daniel was a finalist for the UK News Writer of the Year award, before going on to work as a senior reporter on a daily newspaper and feature writer for The Culture Magazine. He was the original founder and editor of The Bleed, an independent arts magazine with contributors from the USA and Japan, before he left full-time journalism to research and write a biography of the enigmatic artist, Ezra Maas. In 2019, Daniel's debut novel, *The Unauthorised Biography of Ezra Maas*, was shortlisted for *The Guardian*'s Not The Booker Prize. His current whereabouts are unknown ('Daniel James Writer – About').

This short description seamlessly blends the writer with his fictitious persona, as it includes James's pursuit of the enigmatic artist Ezra Maas. Furthermore, the final line ('His current whereabouts are unknown') echoes his fate in the novel. This line is no longer on the website (as of April 2022), which suggests that the recent publishing developments (the 2022 new edition of the *Unauthorised Biography*) may lead to a return for James also.

The website also features two video-interviews with Bryan

Talbot (British comic book writer) and Dr Claire Nally (associate professor at the Northumbria University), which will be discussed in a later section of this essay.

Although it is not difficult to find pictures of Daniel James on the internet, two of them stand out by their prominence and their composition. The first one is a black and white picture showing only his eyes, as the rest of his face is concealed behind a newspaper. That picture is how the author wishes to be represented, as it is to be found on his website, his various social media accounts, and event posters. The other picture is from a *Bleed* article (also reproduced in the novel and accessible through the Maas Wikipedia page). Contrary to the previous one, Daniel's eyes are redacted, and only the bottom of his face is visible. Those two partial, yet complementary images suggest that James's identity is also fragmented. The former conveys mystery, intrigue, and control; the latter conveys anonymity, shame, and erasure.

b. Foregrounding the missing artist

A Wikipedia page thoroughly dealing with the figure of Ezra Maas recently surfaced on the internet. From the onset, one can notice that the page is unlike any other, starting with the logo.

(left: Wikipedia logo; right: Maas's Wikipedia logo)

The use of different (no doubt meaningful symbols) and the slightly blurry look of the logo point towards the constant negotiation between reality (or what looks real, familiar) and the fiction, thus treading the realm of the uncanny.[38]

Wikipedia perfectly lends itself to an encyclopedic and seemingly factual rewriting of the novel. The page condenses the events of Maas's life and presents them in chronological order, which allows readers to have a clearer overview of his story. A major difference between the novel and the Wikipedia page is that the latter is no longer polyphonic: a single voice replaces that of James, Anonymous, and the numerous characters talking about Maas in the novel (even though the author of the page makes numerous references to James's work).

The existence of the page, however, as factual as it may look, raises the important issue of authorship. Maas is brought to the forefront, yet still largely remains a mystery; James is mentioned as biographer on several occasions (in a rather favourable manner), but the events of his life and his pursuit of Maas are not. The encyclopedic and thorough nature of the page (numerous footnotes, quotes, references to authors, lengthy bibliography, etc.) are in keeping with Anonymous's literary identity in the novel and suggests that they may be the author of the page. The change of medium arguably changes the power dynamic between the three protagonists: James is rendered more passive and secondary,

---

38. Defined as 'a fundamental insecurity brought about by a "lack of orientation", a sense of something new, foreign, and hostile invading an old, familiar, customary world' (Vidler 1).

Maas has a more prominent space although not a more prominent agency. The author of the page (I argue, Anonymous) now has the status of author (rather than that of owner as mentioned in the novel).

This new and dynamic medium also makes it possible for another figure to take on a more active role: that of the reader. Novels such as the *Unauthorised Biography* can be considered what N. Katherine Hayles calls hypertext, that is to say a text that has 'multiple reading paths; […] that is chunked together in some way; and [in which there is] some kind of linking mechanism that connects the chunks together so as to create multiple reading paths' (Hayles 21), insofar as they allow for a dynamic exploration through the extensive use of footnotes. As far as *The Unauthorised Biography* is concerned, it requires a movement of back and forth between the footnotes and the main body of text, and might prompt some (the most thorough) readers to do extra research in order to understand the numerous references to historical events, people, art movements, scientific theories, etc. present in the novel.

However, the hypertextual effect hits in full force with the Maas Wikipedia page and its hyperlinks. They offer readers the possibility to explore different types of resources:

(1) Other Wikipedia pages: those pages are usually related to complex topics (e.g. quantum physics, religious apocrypha), artistic movements (e.g. Fluxus, Oulipo), and historical figures (e.g. David Bowie, Tomas Pynchon). They function the same way as Anonymous's lengthy footnotes and allow readers to get a more thorough understanding of the material at end and research conducted by James in order to write his novel.

(2) Articles: James already uses newspaper clippings in the novel to heighten a sense of reality within the fiction, thus highlighting his complex relationship to truth in the process. As mentioned in the novel: 'James has attracted considerable criticism during his controversial career as a journalist. His writing [...] sees the line between fact and fiction blurred in an unorthodox hybrid' (James 3).

(3) Videos: the page also contains hidden links to videos. Two of them are available on James's website and Youtube channel, and three are available on the Maas Foundation Website and on the pig's Youtube channel (more on those below).

In many ways, the Wikipedia page functions as a Maas encyclopedia, where all the material available about the artist is made available outside the realm of the novel. This new medium allows readers to conduct their own investigation, freed from James and Anonymous's mediation.

On top of a Wikipedia page devoted to Maas, his Foundation possesses its very own website, which contains very minimal biographical data. In fact, only his date of birth is mentioned: '1 January 1950' ('The Maas Foundation – About'), and this alone has been contradicted by many. James highlights in the biography that Maas may have been born in November 1947, and, in true Maas fashion, neither can be (dis)proved, since 'his original birth certificate was destroyed in a fire' (James 31). By only providing that one (debated) piece of information, as simple as a birth date and place, yet as controversial as the rest, the Foundation sets the tone. The website is still active and updated, as shown by the work list, which now contains an entry for 2021: 'Daniel James is Dead' ('The Maas Foundation – Work'). Aside from the about section, the website contains two other interesting ones: 'work' and 'private'. The 'work' page lists Maas's works spanning from 1966 to 2021. The lengthy list allows readers to revisit Maas's life through five decades of work. In this case, the novel can be used as a reading key in order to situate the works in Maas's life and subsequently understand the context of those works.[39] There are undoubtedly many ways to 'read' and interpret this work list, and it surely is too ambitious an undertaking to conduct within the scope of this paper. However, let's consider the following threads as an illustration of the richness that lies in it.

Several references allude to disorders affecting children (Lesch-Nyhan syndrome, Riley-Day syndrome) or disorders caused by a brain injury (Landau-Kleffner, aphasia, hemispatial neglect, prosopagnosia). Both Ezra and his brother Daniel allegedly sustained a fall, which may have led them to experiencing such issues. Although Maas attributes much of his 'specialness' to being born that way (a.o. his synesthesia), his work list suggests an interest in understanding afflictions

---

[39] The references are too numerous to detail here, but they mostly deal with the following topics: Greek and Roman antiquity/mythology; religions; psychoanalysis; philosophy; and sciences. The scientific concerns could be further divided into different categories: physics; neurology; quantum mechanics. Other concerns include: duality and the self, and metafiction.

caused by brain injuries. In this case, the work list might suggest possible disorders Maas (or his brother, if he survived) may have been living with as a consequence of their fall: inability to perceive stimuli from one side of the body (hemispatial neglect), inability to comprehend of formulate language (aphasia, Landau-Kleffner syndrom), seizures (Landau-Kleffner).

Other syndromes from the list highlight Maas's interest for duality and identity: Capgrass syndrome refers to the belief that one or several people from our circle have been replaced by look-alikes, while with Cotard's syndrome, the patient may believe that he does not exist, is dead or dying, or conversely have the illusion that they are immortal. Other references to the self and the double include: David's Dream, Eidolon, counterfeit, hall of mirror, alter-ego, Voigt-Kampf, Daniel, Quinn.

Another important multimedia extension of the novel, as mentioned previously, is the videos. Brian Talbot recounts his experience working with Maas, their chaotic still-born novella project, while also suggesting that he was indirectly the influence of much of the counterculture of the 60's and the 70's. Dr Claire Nally discusses the figure of Ezra Maas as a highly postmodern figure and the challenge of attempting a biography on such a multi-facetted and elusive individual. She states: 'it wouldn't surprise me if Ezra Maas had embedded all manner of… of kind of clues in his work to kind of suggest his return […] I suspect there's a lot of clues in the work that suggest that this isn't the end of it' (Nally).

While the last entry in Maas's work list seems to confirm Nally's statement ('2021 Daniel James is Dead'), the only 'work' available to the readers are the three videos embedded on the Maas Foundation website. The section entitled 'Private' leads the reader to mysterious messages accompanied by ominous music:

['Maas Foundation – private']

['Maas Foundation – waiting']

Three of the words in the quotation above are clickable ('everything,' 'hope,' and 'truth'), and lead to three different paths. Each one consists of a mysterious artwork paired with a quote, and leads to a video on a YouTube channel named 'The Pig' (a reference to one of the masked kidnappers from the novel). Three videos in total can be viewed: 'Doorways,' 'Numbers,' and 'Video.' 'Video' features a TV screen with blueish static (reminiscent of Lynch's *Fire Walk We Me* opening sequence), as well as the words 'DON'T – WATCH – THE – FILM.' (a reference to Maas's film *Absence*). 'Doorways' is filmed in the first person as someone walks through the empty rooms of an abandoned building in ruins. This time, the words say 'HE – IS – WAITING.' That video also features numbers: 2, 3 and 8, as well as a graffiti stating 'Maas Lives.' 'Numbers' is the most complex, as it contains a long list of small numbers, as well as three big ones: 2, 3 and 8 again, inserted in the middle of the following list: 3, 29, 17, 3, 18, 27, 6, 15, 4, 5, 25, 32, 11 / 11, 9, 24, 34, 8, 26, 7, 16. The noise that punctuates the appearance of the numbers is reminiscent of the countdown before old films.

In keeping with the new edition's desire to give the readers an immersive experience,[40] pictures anchor places, people, and events in our reality. Aside from the vivid description of the group photo at 't Gulden Vlies (Bruges), actual pictures are (and will be) featured in the novel. The picture below, for instance, depicts a Parisian optician's façade tagged with the words 'Maas Live' (just like in the 'Doorway' video). Upon visiting the place, however, the graffiti was not there anymore. Maybe it never was. Maybe someone wiped the wall clean before I could make it there. By openly making reality and fiction overlap, James invites the reader to close the book and go out into the world to seek – and hopefully find – traces of Maas outside the realm of the novel.

[40.] This aspect of the new edition would deserve an entire essay itself.

[left: L'opticien's façade in Paris with the 'Maas Lives' graffiti; right: a proud yet disappointed fan of the novel in front of the very same façade, now wiped clean]

CONCLUSION

In this essay, I have showed how *The Unauthorised Biography Ezra Maas* subverts literary genres and conventions in order to create a work that blurs the boundaries between fiction and reality. The use of the metaphysical detective genre, the pseudo-biography, and the historiographical metafiction creates the ideal backdrop for an investigation into a mysterious figure that turns into an investigation into the nature of identity and narrative, thus expending the scope of the novel in the process. While such postmodern metafictional works usually rely on an open-ending or a circular narrative to suggest the potential of never-ending play, James opens the narrative to the world wide web. This allows him to realise the full potential of his Work as Assemblage through the creation of a multimedia rhizome of interconnected nodes around the novel. Those nodes supplement, remediate, enrich, contradict, etc. one another, thus upholding the promise of never-ending play and providing the reader with the same intoxicatingly dangerous, yet addictive experience of literary detection as its protagonist. The rhizome also proposes different entry points into the narrative across different media and the possibility to approach the novel through a different lens, thus deconstructing traditional narrative conventions. The result is a complete and uncompromising collaborative work, no longer only a literary assemblage of genres, text types, and media, but also of individuals. At the end of the foreword, Anonymous tells the reader: 'The next chapter belongs to you' (James 2). His words take on a whole new meaning thanks to the novel crossing the boundary of the bounded artefact – a pandora box spilling its cursed content, overflowing the limits of its pages, ink turning into blood as it seeps into our reality, getting a hold of the readers, forcing the pen into their hands, awaiting the next chapter. No longer witness, they become active participants, writers in their own right, not blurring the boundaries but breaking them altogether, shattering the mirror of illusion standing between writer and reader, between reality and fiction, between story and history, becoming aware that one has been the other all along. That none of it matters because all of it matters, that such formulaic genre as the detective story can and will continue to offer refreshing new ways to approach and appropriate literature. *The Unauthorised Biography of Ezra Maas*, as a work that is as 'mad, bad, and dangerous to know' (Nally), yet irresistible, does exactly that.

Allen, Graham. *The New Idiom: Intertextuality*. Routledge, 2000.

Auster, Paul. *The New-York Trilogy*. Faber and faber, 1987.

Bernstein, Stephen. '"The Question is the Story Itself": Postmodernism and Intertextuality in Auster's New-York Trilogy.' *Detecting Texts*, edited by Patricia Merivale and Susan Elizabeth Sweeney, University of Pennsylvania Press, 1999, pp. 134–156.

Daniel James Writer. danieljameswriter.com [accessed 20 Apr. 2022].

Dechêne, Antoine. '"Unreadable" Texts: From the Metaphysical Detective Story to the Metacognitive Mystery Tale.' Springer International Publishing Langue, 2018.

Dubois, Jacques. *Le roman policier ou la modernité*. Fernand Nathan, 1992.

Graulund, Rune. 'Text and Paratext in Mark Z. Danielewski's *House of Leaves*.' *Word & Image*, vol. 22, no. 4, 2006. pp. 379–89.

Hayles, N. Katherine. 'The Transformation of Narrative and the Materiality of Hypertext.' *Narrative*, vol. 9, no. 1, 2001, pp. 21–39.

Holloway, Mara. 'Interview with Daniel James: Looking for Ezra.' *The ECHO Review Online*. theechoreviewonline.com/articles/literature/interview-with-Daniel-James [accessed 19 Apr. 2022].

Hutcheon, Linda. *A Poetics of Postmodernism: History, Theory, Fiction*. Routledge, 1988.

James, Daniel. *The Unauthorised Biography of Ezra Maas*. Valley Press, 2022.

Karoui-Elounelli, Salwa. 'Self-Parody and the Aesthetics of Literary Transgression in John Hawkes's *An Irish Eye* and Thomas Pynchon's *Inherent Vice.*' *The Poetics of Genre in the Contemporary Novel*, edited by Tim Lanzendörfer, Lexington Books, 2017.

Letort, Delphine. *Du film noir au néo-noir: Mythes et stéréotypes de l'Amérique (1941–2008)*. L'Harmattan, 2010.

Merivale, Patricia, and Susan Elizabeth Sweeney, editors. *Detecting Texts: The Metaphysical Detective Story from Poe to Postmodernism*. University of Pennsylvania Press, 1999.

--. 'The Game's Afoot: On the Trail of the Metaphysical detective Story.' *Detecting Texts*, edited by Patricia Merivale and Susan Elizabeth Sweeney, University of Pennsylvania Press, 1999.

Nally, Claire. 'The Maas Tapes Vol 1 #2 with Dr Claire Nally.' Youtube, uploaded by Daniel James, 15 Feb. 2020, youtube.com/watch?v=MdeHG8QOJus.

Nealon, Jeffrey T. 'Work of the Detective, Work of the Writer: Auster's *City of Glass.*' *Detecting Texts*, edited by Patricia Merivale and Susan Elizabeth Sweeney, University of Pennsylvania Press, 1999.

Skare, Roswitha. 'Paratext – a Useful Concept for the Analysis of Digital Documents?' *Proceedings from the Document Academy*, vol. 6, no. 1. 2019.

The Maas Foundation. 2017, ezramaas.com [accessed 20 Apr. 2022].

'The Maas Foundation – private.' The Maas Foundation, ezramaas.com/#private [accessed 20 Apr. 2022].

'The Maas Foundation – waiting.' The Maas Foundation, ezramaas.com/#waiting [accessed 20 Apr. 2022].

Vidler, Anthony. 'The Architectural Uncanny.' *Fen-om*. fen-om.com/theory/theory159.html [accessed 20 Apr. 2022].

The Mythmaker:
Ezra Maas and the
Value of Art[41]

Dr. Daniel Barnes

Nobody knows more about how to generate value in art than Ezra Maas. It is done by sleight of hand, smoke and mirrors, and not a little conjuring. Tonight, I'm going to talk to you about that value of art: what it is, how it is made, and how Maas embodies it by making a myth of himself.

It is a common misconception that the value of art resides in its being a product or a commodity. I hope to disavow you of that notion. The value of art, as we shall see, is a spectacular construct, a cosmos with the artist at its centre. Ezra Maas is the quintessential illustration of this conception of value.

When we talk about the value of art, we are really talking about two distinct, but interlinked, strands.[42] On the one hand, there is price tag attached to a work of art, which is its economic value, and on the other hand, there is the

------

41. The following is the transcript of a talk I gave at the University of Oxford on 7th January 2020 to mark Ezra Maas' 70th birthday. This written transcript has provided the opportunity to add notes clarifying certain points whereas doing so in the original lecture would have interrupted the flow.

significance of the work in a fundamentally aesthetic sense, its *cultural value*.

On the primary market – that is, galleries selling new artworks for the first time – the price tends to reflect the artist's popularity, which is just the artworld's way of expressing a sort of inverted supply and demand, whereby the greater the demand the higher the price, almost without regard for the status of supply. Take a famously prolific and egregiously expensive artist like Damien Hirst, for example: it doesn't matter how many Spot Paintings his studio can churn out, since the price is determined by demand – greater demand begets higher prices, and if supply cannot match it, then collectors are gleefully placed on a waiting list. Supply is perversely divorced from demand when it comes to setting prices. The other factor that plays into primary market prices is, of course, profit: galleries tend to split sales 50/50 with artists, so 50% of the sale price needs to cover overheads and generate a healthy profit.

On the secondary market – action houses, for example, or anywhere that sells artworks that have previously been owned – the story is a little different. While the primary market sets a baseline price, such that you cannot get a brand new medium-sized Hirst through his galleries for less than £500,000, secondary market prices are significantly driven

---

42. This distinction and its consequences are the subject of my book, *The Value Industry: Reflections on Art, Money and Celebrity* (KDP/NewThey Publishing, 2019). In this lecture, I took the opportunity to elucidate somewhat, so the forgoing should act to compliment rather than to repeat what I have already said.

by a more traditional model of supply and demand. As such, the notion of scarcity is crucial to the secondary market, since when a Picasso or a Rothko comes up at Christie's, the price is function of the fact that it is the only one available at that moment, with no guarantee of it or another one becoming available at any time soon. And in its turn, this creates demand, which drives prices up further still.[43]

We call this strand of value, which is merely and only about the amount of money that changes hands in the commerce of art, economic value. Like much anything else in the world of capitalism, economic value can be manipulated more or less deliberately: it is not unknown for artists, or their gallerists, to buy back their works at auction in order to 'protect prices', which is the artworld's way of creating demand by constricting supply; and primary market galleries will, as a marketing strategy, normally raise artist prices with each new exhibition, quite regardless of whether the artists has done anything to merit it, because the increased price suggests increased popularity and increased demand.

Maas knows all about economic value.[44] He's manipulated the market more than most to ensure that he's in control of supply, making work in whatever medium takes his fancy and unfurling it to a slack-jawed, ravenous market. But, in

---

[43.] For a first-hand account of the art market, see Don Thompson, *The $12 Million Stuffed Shark: The Curious Economics of Contemporary Art* (Arum Press, 2008).

[44.] I refer to Maas in the present tense partly for theatrical effect – my audience are all determined to keep Maas alive – but also because the Ezra Maas Foundation is now merely a proxy for the man himself.

a sense, he's not in control of demand, which is itself off the scale and has been since year zero.

On the other hand, we have cultural value, which is conceptually slippery compared to economic value, but by that token somewhat richer in insight.[45] Cultural value encompasses all those elements which we think have nothing to do with money (although of course they do); it is a way of articulating the reasons we value art as a human pursuit of the highest order.

The contribution of an artwork or an artist's body of work to the ongoing narrative of art history, the way it pushes the boundaries or challenges convention, or its endurance through the generations, the column inches it generates, the rich critical prose it inspires, and the museum collections it fortifies. These are all example of cultural value. The classic example is the inestimable value of Marcel Duchamp's *Fountain*, which invented the readymade and heralded the birth of conceptual art – so seismic we would hardly have culture without it.

The thing about cultural value is that it is not difficult to predict which works will have it and which will not. One would think it was quite obvious in 1917 that *Fountain* would have lasting value to human visual culture. The same should be said for any given Caravaggio, *The Last Supper*, *Las*

[45.] It is worth noting that the distinction itself is derived from Isabelle Graw, *High Price: Art between the Market and Celebrity Culture* (Sternberg Press, 2009), where she uses the terminology 'market value' and 'symbolic value'. See *The Value Industry*, pp. 3–4 for an explanation of why I changed the terminology.

Meninas, and *Blue Poles* and *Guernica*. A seasoned professional, an acute aesthetic eye, a bristling intellect knows – almost instinctively – when they are in the presence of greatness.[46] The pre-theoretical obviousness of this puts one in mind of Sir Nicholas Serota refusing to buy up Hirsts and Emins in the early 90s when they were cheap because he couldn't see their enduring significance.[47]

Essentially, this sense of cultural value is a measure of the work's importance, which is nowhere near as subjective a judgment nor an impossible task from the vantage point of history as people tend to suppose, but no time for that now. It was obvious when Maas burst on to the art scene that his work was important and that it would have enduring significance in reshaping the cannon of 20th Century art. And the same goes for Picasso, Warhol, Hockney, Kiefer…

Another pervasive sense of cultural value, which is closer to the hearts and minds of the art-seeking public, is the way we as individuals value art as an edifying aesthetic and intellectual experience. Art, after all, is an experience we seek because it enriches our lives in some way: sometimes it moves us to consider life and the world in a whole new way, or it reflects or challenges our thoughts and experiences, or it simply gives a distinct kind of aesthetic pleasure that nothing

----

46. Those who are sceptical of the professional's ability to see that which they might think is both subjective and unknowable would do well to acquaint themselves with Malcolm Gladwell's theory of 'thin slicing' in *Blink* (Allen Lane, 2005).

47. Sir Nicholas Serota was Director of the Tate Galleries, England, from 1988 to 2017.

else can deliver. This, one might say, is the true and pure value of art. And, crucially, it is the sense of value which scarcely touches the sticky-fingered business of money, for no gallery, auction house nor artist can put a price on the majesty of the way you and I feel in the presence of the art we admire. It is, as Nietzsche said, 'only as an aesthetic phenomenon that existence and the world are eternally justified.'[48] That is Nietzsche's way of reminding us that life, with its manifold trials and hardships, is rendered worthwhile by our aesthetic engagements with art, which is a rather pithy way of summing up cultural value.

At the beginning, I suggested that the strands of value have the same source. Now that we have elucidated those strands a bit, we can see Maas is the quintessential demonstration of that claim. It is tempting to think that the artwork is the source of its value. After all, it is the painting or the sculpture, or the video or installation, that changes grubby hands on the open market, so we think that must be the locus of value. However, consider that artworks, as artefacts, are often (or usually) made of relatively inexpensive, everyday materials. If we valued them as objects, they'd be worth very little indeed. There must, then, be something more, something that transfigures a conglomeration of stuff into the holy sacrament of art, just in the same way that there is some sleight of hand that transfigures the ordinary plastic, metal and glass of the iPhone into a hallowed modern obsession worth hundreds of pounds.[49] In the case of the iPhone, it is clear that its ubi-

---

[48.] Friedrich Nietzsche, *The Birth of Tragedy*, §5. In *Basic Writings of Nietzsche*, translated and edited by Walter Kaufman (Modern Library, 1963).

quity and undeniable utility is part of the answer, but the other – much more powerful – part is the Apple brand itself.

And so it is with art, such that value – cultural and economic – derives from the power of the brand, which is, of course, the artist. When we venerate a work of art, we do so as an extension of and a product of the artist, for it is their personal brand, whatever that may be, that imbues the artefact – which, remember, in and of itself, is made of everyday stuff – with the indelible value that we ascribe to it. Maas' works are, for sure, great works of art as aesthetic phenomena, but they are only valuable in the precise way that they are, to both economics and culture, because they are by Maas.

Think of any artist and you will see that the value of their work is a function of how they have constructed their brand, of who and what they are in the public eye. This process is always a species of mythmaking. Artists mythologise themselves, build a wall around their true, everyday selves, if you'll allow me such crude terminology for a moment, to construct an artist-persona who coheres with the art so sublimely that the two are indistinguishable.

This is necessary, perhaps, because artists as mere people often do not cohere with their art. One only need consider the irascible, philandering, abusive drunk, Jackson Pollock, to see a character which is at odds with the sublime genius of his paintings. A mythologised self was needed – and so Pollock became a transcendental free spirit who took to Long

---

49. I am alluding here, with talk of transfigurations and sacraments, to Arthur C Danto's discussion of Warhol in 'The Artworld' (*Journal of Philosophy* LXI, 1964, pp. 571–584).

Island to paint in the fresh majesty of the great outdoors – to cohere with the ground-breaking, mesmerising work he produced. After all, there's nothing ground-breaking or mesmerising about a drunk who cheats on his wife, so it seems entirely reasonable that Pollock, his people and the press had to construct a Pollock-persona who could plausibly have the great paintings attributed to him.

Thus, the artist's myth becomes their brand. Gilbert & George are two people, one artist in pristine suits who eschew the everyday to focus on their art; Julian Schnabel is the trail-blazing Ernest Hemmingway of art; Tracey Emin is Mad Tracey from Margate... and so on. Maas is the multi-talented polymath whose difficult childhood haunts him in silence and whose mysterious withdrawal from the artworld, left behind a spectacular legacy and an unfinished masterwork.

The myth of Maas is the reason the work has any value at all precisely because he is the source of value, the first cause of the artefact and the architect of all aesthetic experiences the work has to offer. When people buy a Maas, they are self-consciously paying money for a slice of that myth, to possess it as if they possess a sliver of the man's soul. When we stand before a Maas, we are struck by the hands of the great man weaving magic right before our very eyes.

Perhaps nobody will ever truly know Maas, mired as he is in a myth of his own making and further muddied by the voracious clouds of modern celebrity that continue to engulf him. Daniel James' wonderful biography comes closer than anything else to untangling the man Maas and the myth he created, but it ultimately remains unenlightening because Maas, like any artist worth his salt, does not want to be known apart from the mythology.[50] It doesn't matter, though. We still have the artworks, and that's what matters because Maas lives on through them. We will always know the myth of Mass, built by himself, perpetuated by the press and capitalised up by the artworld, which is the sole and sufficient cause of the near-religious zeal his work continues to inspire.

---

50. Daniel James, *The Unauthorised Biography of Ezra Maas* (Valley Press, 2022).

'Synecdoche, Ezra Maas' or 'How to replace the entire world without anybody noticing'

Matt Cook

When I first read *The Unauthorised Biography of Ezra Maas*, I had no idea what I was getting myself into. At first, I felt I had the measure of it. It was pulling me along via multiple threads – first person narration, found documents, transcripts – each one providing an energetic intermission from a primary, straight-faced account of Ezra Maas' life. This, with its myriad footnotes, was the least stylised and most functional of all these strands. Elegantly and absorbingly written, it was very much the biography that the cover promised, but it was so measured and methodical I wasn't sure what to make of it. The more I read, however, the more I found these were the chapters I needed the most, that I was living in when I put the book down. There were no literary flourishes, no unexpected changes of pace to keep readers engaged in those bits. Just a steady, walking-pace description that sought to reframe everything I presumed to know about western art, culture, philosophy and more in the 20th century.

There are lots of ways to examine this great debut novel, but this is the one I've chosen because it's the one that reverberates at a frequency most in tune with increasingly bizarre and frightening world news at the point of writing.

The Unauthorised Biography of Ezra Maas takes you through the last 80 or so years, steadily rebuilding it for you with a huge negative space at the centre. It presents a kind of hypothesis: what if most of the key post war intellectual developments and artistic moments had been touched some- how by a person – or at least the idea of a person – that you've never even heard of. The titular Ezra Maas. Enigmatic child prodigy and polymath. If it happened and it mattered, he was there. The result is a giant presence, at once omni- present and yet absolutely ethereal. It takes a deft touch to do this, and it has to be detailed to work, although the scope is so vast it still becomes a whistle-stop tour in places. While it does rewrite history, it does not really change events or suggest they happened differently to the way a reader prob- ably understands them. It simply explains – in the calm and measured tone of voice employed in the biography chapters – that the energy that impacted them was all aligned around a singular man-shaped space. It stains them all with a single set of fingerprints.

By the time we reach the denouement, all these component threads have collided, and this suggestion of Maas is faced down by Daniel James (the journalist) in a bewildering vortex of conceptual writing. There is danger in the book, we know that from the cover itself. Constant, malevolent creeping violence that stalks James and overwhelms him, obliterating him it would seem. But beneath the physical threat of the Maas Foundation is a much more horrifying existential threat. Any attempt to look directly at the thing being pursued is as futile as it is perilous. The details are inconsequential. The point is, you can't see it. To try is to willingly enter the abyss.

Imitation and authenticity have many precedents in art, and no one obsesses about it more than Charlie Kaufman. Like his theatre director in *Synecdoche, New York*, the film reviewer in his novel *Antkind* – every detail of the real world must be painstakingly reconstructed. Emphasis on pain.

It reminds me of a fascination I've long had with Capgras Syndrome. Capgras sufferers irrationally believe that familiar people around them have been replaced by doppelgängers. To them, the person is like the original in every respect, the only way they can tell they are not the real thing is that they 'feel' it. They can tell something is *off*. This instinct for danger and for truth is our most precious commodity and it always has been. Does this food smell okay? Can I trust this person with my kids? It comes down to your gut. But how does that work when you scale things up to a societal level? When compound levels of trust are required at scale over huge periods of time?

As Joseph Goebbels told it, the bigger the lie, the more people are likely to believe it. And Daniel James (the author), has attempted to rebuild nothing less than the world to be exactly as we know it, except for that blind spot in the centre. This constant stepping outside of itself requires constant effort and patience, which is why, even though the dramatic narrative revolves around Daniel James (the journalist)'s reckoning with Maas, the impact of the book comes from the reader's reckoning with a world rebuilt so carefully around them.

I found the effects of this sleight of hand to be devastating, precisely because of its patient, methodical, rigorous approach.

(To clarify: the world that is rebuilt is one comprised of particular cultural and artistic touchpoints. Every key mystery, every artistic movement of significance – and many more that aren't mentioned, simply by implication – are woven into the fabric. It is not the physical world, so much as what we take reality to be thanks to countless revered artistic expressions of it. It is the scaffolding that holds up a certain western worldview, an intuition for how these things all connect. It is the very act of connecting them in order to blow those connections up that hollows you out.)

WHICH BRINGS US ON TO BORGES

It is impossible not to feel the presence of Jorge Luis Borges in all of this. Borges created disarming worlds filled with mirrors and uncertainty. In my personal favourite of his stories he even had a small army of people create an entire fictional world – Tlum. But he only ever exercised this practice in bite-size morsels, famously claiming there wasn't really any point in bothering to do it at scale. In *Ficciones*, he wrote:

> Why spend 300 hundred pages on a subject that in a chat would occupy only 5 minutes? This is way better to imagine that a novel exists, than write a critic on it of less than 10 pages and the critic of this unexisting novel will itself be a fictional short story (Borges).

He also said that his reluctance to write a novel came down to two things, his *'incorrigible laziness'* and the fact that he wanted to keep his eye on the story throughout, impossible in a longer piece.

> With a novel, one sees the whole when one has
> forgotten many details, when it has organised itself
> as a whole in the mind's eye (Borges).

This is really interesting, since conceptually it amounts to the same thing. But the passage of time is that much longer, which means the reader has to work harder and remember more. You build the experience in a different way – one can see the distance one has travelled. Both novels and short stories should leave you changed, however, the longer it takes to read, the more that life and the world will have also changed you in that time. A lot more of your cells will have replaced themselves by the time you finish *Ulysses*, than, say, *Two Gallants*.

I couldn't help reading *Ezra Maas* as a direct product of that logic. What if you did pursue those kind of artistic questions at scale? What if that short sharp shock of existential sleight of hand wasn't short or sharp, but steadily and rigorously drawn out and rendered with real scrutiny?

To follow every thread to its conclusion, to create a logic for every micro-narrative that is perfectly realistic and convincing, is no small thing. But the result mechanically disarms you the more you ingest. As I said, it wasn't instantaneous, for me. It took a while for the feeling to overtake me. Instead of feigning and suggesting these ideas to cut into your brain with Borgesian precision, it slowly winds you in with details. The detective narrative appears to contain the threat and the danger, but it is the background – rendered by gaslight – that really fucks you up.

It is by deceiving you layer upon layer upon layer that it undoes you. And why it so well echoes the world we now find ourselves living in.

If we didn't know it when Daniel James (both of them) started writing *The Unauthorised Biography of Ezra Maas*, we sure as shit know it now. We are living in an information war, driven by all manner of engines, from Facebook to Russian troll farms. Nobody knows what is going on any more, so they cling to the basics. To what they hold dear. To what they *used* to feel certain – in their guts – was 'true'.

Our world as we know it has been entirely rebuilt as notion. It is no accident that art is the very core of *The Unauthorised Biography of Ezra Maas* – every artistic act is rebuilding the world as a notion, after all. But we now perceive global events through a digital lens that pretends to offer the real thing. We all have an understanding of the shared material space and its rules, both physical and human. The collective super ego is working overtime, addressing shared received wisdom for values and connections of all kinds that are increasingly incompatible and unsound.

When values are seen to be trashed and history unjustly rewritten, people have very powerful visceral reactions, a process laid extremely bare in 2016 with the Brexit referendum and the election of Donald Trump. James has done the same here, undermining our Ur cultural heroes and touch points – the very idea of cultural touch points, the idea of the sanctity and value of art, as well as casting shadow over our greatest visionaries. Everyone and everything is subservient to an invisible figure who transcends them. If you glue all these different valued components together with nothing, you undo them at a base level. Like Borges looking into a mirror, we pass into another dimension.

It's still baffling how certain world leaders can lie with such apparent shamelessness and yet retain the trust of their supporters. Politicians lying is nothing new, but the nakedness is. It shows a particular quality of 'truth' in stark and painful relief. These liars have become fiction writers in the exact way Camus described. They tell their followers what is clearly a lie in order to uncover what viscerally feels true. It is the Capgras effect in reverse. The gut reaction trumps the cognitive one every time. It's terrifying and it's insane, but then storytelling in itself – willing submission of one's core emotional makeup to the whims of someone else's imagination – is not, I would argue, a wholeheartedly sane act. It is something we learn to do with trusted, familiar people, as children. The people we know in our hearts and our guts would never ever lie to us unless it was in our best interest.

The digital world is now represented through trillions of borrowed associations, and it is being rebuilt constantly. The Tlonic world-builders are at work en masse, fabricating human opinion as readily as rewriting historical facts. The fault lines of the collective super ego are laid bare for those who choose to see them.

I felt relieved after finishing *Ezra Maas*, simply because I recognised my own 'real world' again and that feeling of recognition was incredibly reassuring. I could tell the real from the unreal. At least it felt that way. But each time I go online I feel the exact opposite feeling. The fabric of shared human understanding is being woven in real-time, before our very eyes. We cannot ever truly know who is doing it. So why shouldn't it be Ezra Maas?

Through the looking-glass: Ezra Maas, the man in the mirror

Dr. Magdalena Harper

> If I had a world of my own, everything would
> be nonsense. Nothing would be what it is,
> because everything would be what it isn't.
> – Lewis Carroll

> [N]othing around me and without
> me nothing other than nothing... I came,
> then, from eternity and head into eternity.
> – Jean Paul

In her seminal paper on *The Unauthorised Biography of Ezra Maas* (James, 2022), Ruth Horowitz argues: 'Ezra is the name which Daniel James's trauma took. It was never about Ezra, it was about Daniel. Except it was never about him either' (Horowitz 44). This quote – especially the second part – has stirred numerous debates in the literary and academic spheres, has been quoted and misquoted repeatedly, and still keeps many wondering. As Gus Van Der Valk cried out at the end of a symposium on New Journalism: 'What the hell is that even supposed to *mean*?'[51] Despite the rather informal tone of the comment, he asked the burning question that was on everybody's lips. Since Horowitz's untimely death,[52] which occurred only a few days after she finished writing the article, nobody has been able to understand what she really meant by that evasive statement. Her daughter, Michelle Duncan-Horowitz, stated in an interview for *Time Magazine*: 'My mother was a very secretive person. It got worse when she got a hold of that goddamn book... I'm sorry. [...] It has been a rough four weeks. What I mean to say is, she seemed to only live for that. When I heard that she had died the day after submitting her paper to the journal, I freaked out. You see what I mean? She literally lived for *that*' (███████ 36).[53]

This paper does not seek to assign yet another wrongful meaning to Horowitz's statement, but rather to examine how such a statement embodies the struggle and unease surrounding James's *Unauthorised Biography*. More specifically, it will address how such notions as authorship and identity, and

------

[51.] Van Der Valk denies ever saying that, although many witnesses have reported the sentence word for word. However, none of them were available to confirm it.

[52.] Ruth Horowitz (1952–2020), emeritus professor in English Literature at the University of Exeter, was found dead at her home in Dorchester. She reportedly died of a heart attack in the middle of her living room. She was found a few days later by her maid. Other accounts suggest a much darker fate: she might have died during a robbery gone wrong, allegedly plotted by none other than the aforementioned maid.

even the very nature of narrative, are constantly called into question in an endless mirror effect.

GENESIS OR CHIAROSCURO

And God saw the light, that it was good:
and God divided the light from the darkness.
– Genesis

The term chiaroscuro – literally 'light-dark' –, is a painting technique defined as the 'clear tonal contrasts which are often used to suggest the volume and modeling of the subjects depicted' ('Chiaroscuro'). In 'The Fine Arts of Ezra Maas', Paola Moretti makes a case that…

> … although the chiaroscuro technique is nowhere
> to be found in [Maas's] paintings, it is, I argue,
> very much there for those who can look. Oftentimes,
> one merely sees. One cannot simply see Maas's work,
> one has to look deeper, and what one sees when one
> does is beyond words (Moretti 13).

Even though she has a point, Moretti's article remained largely unnoticed in the field, likely due to her frequent overtly racist stances[54] and her shamelessly hagiographic

---

[53.] This statement is a direct quote from the tape recorded during the interview, transcribed here with Michelle Duncan-Horowitz's permission. Courtesy of ████ ████ , senior editor at *Time Magazine*.

study of Maas's work.[55] In spite of her controversial stances, I find her use of the term chiaroscuro useful when discussing not only Maas's work, but also his life. Chiaroscuro highlights the inevitable bond between light and darkness, a co-dependency that mirrors that between James and Maas. One could simply not exist were it not for the other one (more on that later).[56] Daniel himself seemed aware of the nature of their relationship when he told Samuel Molloy during a phone call: 'I know I can pull this off, Sam. This book... his life... it's mine to write' (James 25). This particular statement has been the subject of much discussion, including an unnecessary convoluted tangent by Jeremiah Loughlin in the independent online journal *L'art pour l'art*.[57]

> James is an ego-maniac. There. I said it. Or should
> I say *write*. Because ever since I – at long last ! –
> managed to swim through James's self-serving swamp
> of outrageously self-absorbed prose, and eventually

[54.] She allegedly dismissed African-American art as 'inferior' during a high-profile symposium in 2006, which might explain the negative reception of her work and her subsequent disappearance from academia in the years that followed. That article is her last.

[55.] This unusual *parti pris* led some people to speculate that Moretti had been hired by the Maas Foundation in an effort to spread a controlled narrative surrounding Maas. One of her former students, ███████████, contacted me about documents proving these allegations. Unfortunately, said documents are likely forgeries.

reached the shore a complete wreck, yet still in one

piece – although I am still not sure that it did not bite off a chunk of my soul in the process – I know that words *matter*. The only sound sentence ever uttered by this pathetic joke of a journalist – and I should know because I lay claim to being one – is that it must be is [sic] *ego* talking. Well, if you ask me – which I always recommend you do – he missed an occasion to shut the hell up. My advice to him would be: try cooking or knitting. These are also perfectly valid past-times (Loughlin).

In spite of being rather delightfully entertaining, such a comment clearly lacks a basic understanding of how metafiction works, or – dare I say – literature in general.[58] Although James himself subscribes to the ego theory, others suggest a deeper connection between him and Maas, which prompted the former to write the latter's biography. Herman Schreiber,[59] for instance, states: '"Daniel", before being our protagonist's first name is the name of Ezra Maas's deceased brother. The parallel between the two Daniels, therefore, is crucial to any further analysis of the novel' (Schreiber 'The Lie' 77).

---

56. That statement itself contradicts the increasingly popular belief according to which the Foundation purely and simply killed Daniel James. It is blatantly obvious that such a conspiracy theory holds no weight. The Foundation *needs* James alive ███████████████████████ ███████████████.

57. Which admittedly reads more like an amateurish blog than an actually respectable attempt at journalism.

Daniel Maas was Ezra's polar opposite: he was 'bookish' (James 33), weakened by 'various illnesses' (Ibid.) and constantly 'indoors' (Ibid.) while Ezra was the 'athletic and outgoing' (Ibid..) one. When Daniel died, however, Ezra 'almost absorb[ed] Daniel's personality into his own' (Ibid) and still referred to him in the present tense, as if he had literally absorbed his brother's essence. Many scholars quote the dedication in his debut novel – 'Daniel will always be with me' (32) – as proof. In 1968, Jenna Harrington, journalist for *Forbes*, commented: 'Maas's debut novel is nothing special, really. And all that fuss about the dedication? Writers have always liked hiding messages. My personal favorite is e.e. cummings's in *No Thanks. That* is a good one' (Harrington 12).[60]

---

58. Several of Loughlin's articles were allegedly turned down by James during his time at *The Bleed*. Prior to his hatred-spewing rant on the *Unauthorised Biography* (which I doubt he read past page 4), Loughlin had already slandered James in a now taken down Twitter thread of the worst possible taste.[a]

   a. In which he allegedly called James a ▮▮▮▮▮ ▮▮▮▮▮ who was so far up ▮▮▮▮▮ that he was incapable of writing a piece that was not even remotely about something other than himself.[b]

   b. What Loughlin fails to understand time and time again is that literature, if anything, is about the pursuit of the self. All writing is, to a certain extent, the desperate answer to a craving for self-knowledge.

59. As will become obvious when reading Schreiber's quotations, he does not believe in Daniel James as a person and constantly refers to him as a character.

Daniel James and Ezra Maas may also share a deep connection, which goes back a longer way than one might expect: according to Cassandra May's (his therapist) notes, James 'had not known his real parents' (James 192). This gap in his story has led a number of people to believe that James was, in fact, Maas's son. Maas was notorious for having had a number of affairs, resulting in the birth of multiple children,[61] as well as one child born from his marriage to Helena.[62] In spite of the constant scrutiny of tabloids, such as *News of the World*,[63] none of the rumors have ever proven to be true, and none of the people suspected to be Maas's children have ever come forward.

[60.] It was later revealed that Harrington had neither read to book nor heard of Ezra Maas prior to writing her review. In 2008, she reminisced about that episode of her career, stating: 'If I remember…? Of course, I do. I was such a cocky b* back then… When I met Maas over a decade later I understood just how misguided my review had been. Lucky me, he was not resentful, and seemed particularly sensitive to 5 feet 9 blonds.'[a]

a. Although this quote is easy to find on the internet, I was unable to track down its source. When I emailed Harrington, her personal assistant let me know that she would never use such self-deprecating language about herself and that the quote was likely apocryphal. When I further insisted to have a word with Harrington about her encounter with Maas, the assistant politely asked me to mind my own business(b). I guess she is not particularly sensitive to petite brown-haired women.

b. I discovered months later that, by the time I emailed her 'assistant', Harrington had been dead for a year.

But there arose in our pathway a shrouded human
figure, very far larger in its proportions than any
dweller among men. And the hue of the skin of the
figure was of the perfect whiteness of the snow.
                    – Poe

Whether he was aware of it or not, James became a literary
device in his own book, embodying the doppelgänger trope
(literally 'walking double'). The term originates from a 1796
novel by Jean Paul entitled *Siebenkäs*, in which an unhappily
married man is urged by his double to fake his own death
(Vardoulakis *The Doppelgänger* unpag.). In Gothic Literature,
the term came to refer to a ghost or a shadow being (Ibid).

As far as *The Unauthorised Biography* is concerned, Maas
can be considered a shadow being, as he never appears in a
physical form, but his presence hovers over the novel and

_____

61. A number of A-list celebrities have been suspected to
be Maas's children, including the actor H█ L█,
the magician D█ B█, and the chess player L█
A█.

62. If, as The Maas Foundation's website suggests, Maas
was born in 1950, he would have been between 25 and
35 when Daniel was born. Although some sources claim
that Daniel James is, in fact, the son of Ezra and Helena,
her birth in 1966 would make her only 10 to 16 years
old when Daniel was born. Highly unlikely though not
impossible.

James's pursuit of the truth. In her article 'Game of Shadows: Ezra vs. Daniel', Vera O'Sullivan points out that 'Daniel running after a shadow is ironic, as the shadow is and will always remain *behind* him' (O'Sullivan 22). I would add to her argument that Daniel being the physical body and Ezra the shadow makes Daniel the *origin* of Ezra.[64] Although this statement arguably plays devil's advocate, it also points to the an essential aspect of the James's pursuit of Maas, namely that it actively participates in his very creation.

Doppelgänger can also refer to 'a character who physically resembles the protagonist' ('Doppelgänger'). This would make Ezra and his brother, who were, on all accounts, 'almost identical' (James 31), fit the description. Although arguably fairly meager, the description made by Suzanne, the owner of ███████████, of Maas also fits with Daniel James's appearance: Maas had 'dark hair, and [...] there was something about his eyes' (47), while James has 'thick dark hair and blue eyes' (50). Furthermore, doppelgängers can also happen to 'have the same name' ('Doppelgänger'). This

---

63. One picture of Helena Maas in particular circulated in 1981, in which she apparently looks like she could be pregnant. As it turns out, the picture is quite blurry and far from convincing.

64. Although Jim Howard, a notoriously mad scientist, once suggested in a self-published paper entitled 'We Have it all Wrong' that 'maybe, shadows are the origin of the beings' (Howard 42). He reportedly tried to strip naked in the middle of a crowded auditorium after screaming that statement and was subsequently politely, then more harshly asked to leave the premises.

latter aspects suggests that James may be Daniel Maas's doppelgänger.[65]

The more one *looks* – as Paola Moretti urged us to do –, the more one notices that James might have been right when he told Samuel Molloy that only he would not, unlike Maas's other biographers,[66] fail in the endeavor. James may indeed very well be the condition for Maas to exist, as suggested by the following statement: 'You will only know that I have succeeded if you don't know who Ezra Maas is [...] If he lives now, it is only in the pages of this book, so I must destroy what I have created. He will die with this text' (James 387).

[65.] Daniel Maas and Daniel James being namesakes is often brought up by supporters of the James-is-Maas's son theory. They view it as Maas's ultimate tribute to his deceased brother. A more extreme strand of supporters – who call themselves the Freemaasons – even suggest that Daniel Maas and Daniel James are the same person. When asked about the logistics of bringing a dead boy back to life – and at a different age at that! – the members have manifested a great deal of disappointment in how little faith I had in Maas's lifework.

[66.] When I called one of Maas's purported biographers, ███████████, he categorically refused an interview. Before hanging up, he said: 'I don't want my name associated with... him... it. You understand? No you don't, of course you don't, you are not deep enough in this... mess. Don't call me again.' When I later called again, I must admit, against ██████'s will, I was informed by the new home-owners that he had hastily moved-out. They had no idea where he had gone.

The doppelgänger trope not only makes sense of the relationship between the characters, but also of James's eventual disappearance. Dimitri Vardoulakis argues that the 'figure of following, accosting, or pursuing' (Vardoulakis, 2010 69) is associated with the doppelgänger and that 'the doppelgänger very often will pursue its other, or be pursued by it, or both' (Ibid.). In this case, James's endeavor is as much his pursuit of Maas as it is Maas's pursuit of James (through the Maas Foundation).[67] Furthermore, such pursuit 'would usually be a prelude to a murder' (Ibid.). This statement suggests that James and Maas's game of cat and mouse could only end in tragedy, although it may not be as literal an ending as murder.

Dan Grüber also believes in a more symbolical understanding of James's 'death'. In '*Doppelgängers* and the Ghost of Goethe', he argues:

> Goethe famously died after encountering his double. The double is, therefore, far from being a familiar and reassuring figure like a (twin) brother would be. The double in this particular case – the *walking* double – roams the earth to take a place that is not his to begin with, but that belongs to the one-who-looks-like-him (Grüber 17).[68]

What this statement suggests as far as Maas and James are concerned is that the latter was meant to disappear once he 'found' the former. In a sense, his pursuit of Maas was a

---

[67.] See the passive-aggressive addition to Maas's work list on the Foundation's website: '2021 Daniel James is Dead.'

prolonged and calculated suicide (rather than murder as suggested above). Cassandra May already mentioned in her 2007 report that she feared that he would 'develop a lust for death' (James 195). In that regard, Maas embodies Daniel's death drive, what Freud called 'thanatos'.

May's comment offers a psychoanalytical explanation to the relationship between the two men. According to Vardoulakis, the doppelgänger embodies the Fichtean concept of the *absolute ego*, a form of God-like expression of the self, which is 'able to feel only absolutely' (Vardoulakis 'The Return' 103). This is very much in line with Maas, whose descriptions in the *Unauthorised Biography* create a patchwork of descriptions

---

68. Grüber died in a similar fashion, after he allegedly encountered his own doppelgänger. His wife, Ginny, stated: 'He came back one day. It was an unusually rainy day that day. He was… irresponsive. As if he was already gone. I later understood, when I found a note on his desk, that he had met with most unsettling circum-stances. Dan had stared at his reflection and it had stared back. The minute their gazes met, Dan was no longer Dan, but a shadow-being that would soon leave the earth. I now long to meet the being that became my husband.' In spite of my efforts, Ginny Grüber categoric-ally refused to share the exact content of the note with me, alleging that she had 'remorselessly burnt it.'[a]

a. Some critics speculate that Ginny, in an attempt to cope with her husband's sudden and unexpected death, developed Capgras's delusion, that is to say: '[t]he delu-sion that family, friends and others have been replaced by imposters' ('Capgras' delusion').

that contradict one another. He is described as a reclusive, discreet, and almost anonymous man; as an eccentric and dangerous addict; as a charming and manipulative liar; as a brilliant and narcissistic genius, etc. In one word: Maas is *absolute*. If one is to believe Donald Houlihan, friend of the Maas family from 1981 onwards, when he says that '[e]verything you've heard about Maas is wrong' (James 325), then one might even argue that Maas is *nothing*. This is supported by Bill Deaver's statement that 'Ezra Maas does not exist' (271).

Maëva Petrakis links the notion of nothingness and that of the doppelgänger in 'Freud and Carroll, the Uncanny and the Mirror'. She argues: '*Nothing*, therefore, becomes the precondition for the subject to cross over. Much like Alice went through the looking-glass, the doppelgänger's nothingness allows for the subject to fully explore the space, even the space that belongs to the Other, and come back changed' (Petrakis 26). In relation to the novel, I would argue that nothingness is not only a condition but also a consequence: when James reaches the end of the novel and is faced with a man who he believes to be Ezra, he is actually faced with absence. Complete and utter *nothingness*.

A contradictory explanation for James's endeavor could be that he wanted to write about Maas in order to give himself the illusion of being, which would, this time, correspond to a lust for life. Daniel's *eros* manifests quite literally in the novel, as he recounts intercourses with several women and hints at many more. One should not forget that Daniel lost all sense of purpose after the tragedy that hit him in 2007.[69] Writing about Maas and subsequently attempting to fully appropriate his alter-ego was arguably a way for him to regain his own sense of self.

Since the *Unauthorised Biography* as a metaphysical novel[70] typically resists interpretation, both readings of James's motives are worth considering. Furthermore, any attempt to stabilize Maas as the origin of James or the other way around are equally bound to fail. Much in the same fashion as M.C. Escher's 'Drawing Hands', the *Unauthorised Biography*'s power lies in the fact that it does not allow for a final answer. The reason is simple: its very foundations rely on instability.

[69.] That year, Daniel James ███████████████████ ████████████. News article about the tragedy are very hard to find, as if somebody had deliberately – in an almost Maasian fashion – tried to erase that part of his life. However, ████████████████████████ have stated that: 'He was shattered, completely. And a shattered man can do unexpected and extreme things. We saw Daniel become someone else entirely, as if his façade had dropped to reveal his true self. In a sense, what happened on that fateful day made Daniel who he truly was, that is to say, a much darker being than we might have thought.' The worst part of this whole story is that ███████████████████████████ ███████████████████████████████████ ██████████████████.

[70.] See Maureen Hosay's article on the metaphysical detective story (this volume).

The whole thing is [...] merely a fantasy.
– Hofstadter

In *I am a Strange Loop* (2007), Douglas Hofstadter discusses M.C. Escher's 'Drawing Hands', a famous lithography illustrating a paradox: one hand drawing the other, yet placed underneath it and being drawn by it at the same time. Hofstadter states:

> [E]ach of the hands is hierarchically 'above' the other! How is that possible? Well, the answer is obvious: the whole thing is merely a drawn image, merely a fantasy. But because it looks so real, because it sucks us so effectively into its paradoxical world, it fools us, at least briefly, *into believing in its reality* [emphasis added] (Hofstadter 119).

Many scholars have drawn a parallel between Hofstadter's famous comment and James's book. In a short article entitled 'The not-so-strange Loop', Schreiber takes a jab at Hofstadter's discussion of the paradox, stating: 'Douglas seems to believe that readers are stupid enough to be caught by such an obvious paradox' (Schreiber 'The not-so-Strange' 11).[71] Hofstadter's PR team issued a short statement in response, coining the phrase 'writing hands' in the process:

> The relationship between Daniel James and Ezra Maas is the same as the one between the drawing hands. The two 'writing hands' create one another, in an endless

loop. It is, therefore, impossible to determine whether James came before Maas, or the other way around. In fact, trying to figure it out is 'stupid'. We hope to emphasize how vain such an endeavor would be (Rochas).

They then proceeded to remind Schreiber that Hofstadter met Maas in the 1980's[72] and that the latter seemed to be very interested in the former's theory about the Escher paradox.[73] As much as I understand Schreiber's remark (after all, he has studied Reader Response Theory extensively[74]), I believe that his conception of the reader is not incompatible with Hofstadter's. Indeed, the latter added to the above

---

[71.] Needless to say, Schreiber does not believe in the suspension of disbelief, which can be defined as a process that '[t]emporarily allow[s] oneself to believe something that is not true, especially in order to enjoy a work of fiction' ('Suspend of Disbelief'). Francesca Suárez studied the concept in relation to that of catharsis, a parallel initially drawn by Aristotle: 'Aristotle believed that the only way one could fully appreciate a work of fiction was to "believe" that said work was real. This is, of course, quite paradoxical, since it suggests that readers can only fully appreciate fiction if they believe it is not what they initially wanted it to be, that is to say, fiction' (Suárez 118). Suárez's statement sounds prophetic in relation to James's endeavor. Never has the reader's desire for the whole story to be true so intense.

[72.] Some sources close to the two men, including █████ ███████, even go as far as to suggest that Hofstadter introduced Helena to Maas.

comment: 'we delight in being taken in by the hoax, hence the picture's popularity' (Hofstadter 119). Nowhere in his article does Schreiber broach the possibility that the reader might be complicit and not victim of the writing hands, thus adding a third hand to the picture, taking an active part in the hoax.

———

73. Witnesses reported that Maas asked Hofstadter to sign his well-worn copy of *Gödel, Escher, Bach* (1979). The two men allegedly formed a lasting friendship from that point on, which led many to believe that Maas directed the 1988 docudrama about Hofstadter 'Victim of the Brain', under the pseudonym Piet Hoenderdos.[a]

a. The film was broadcast in the Netherland in the late 1980's. Following a massive fire in the TV studio of ███████ in ███, the original recording of the film was lost. Luckily a low-quality version was uploaded on Youtube in 2013. Strangely enough, however, the video is only one hour thirty minute-long, while the initial broadcast was five and a half minutes longer. I suspect that the cut can happens at oo:█:33, likely because █ ████████████████████.

74. See for instance: 'Reader's Response Theory and the "stupidity bias"' (1987), 'The Reader is dead, long live the Reader' (1989), and his most recent essay: 'Magician or Fool? Reader Response Theory in the *Unauthorised Biography of Ezra Maas*' (2019).

'Who wrote this book?' he said, once he was
done reading. And he could not believe his eyes
for he saw his own name appear on the cover.
– Thomson

Let us now come back to the late Ruth Horowitz's statement. If the story was neither about Maas nor about James, then who was it about? This question cannot properly be answered without answering another question: whose book is it exactly? As reader, we are introduced to the unauthorised biography of a mysterious figure (Ezra Maas), which also quickly becomes the unreliable autobiography of its author (Daniel James). The heavy-handed yet compelling use of noir tropes to recount James' journey, the suspenseful search for answers, the dense notes on Maas's life and James's search, and the numerous footnotes, might all divert the reader's attention from the fact that there is yet another narrative layer on top of the already complex and skillfully crafted plot: the presence of Anonymous. Jill Simons has extensively commented on the figure of Anonymous in the *Unauthorised Biography*, stating:[75]

[75.] In a chapter (arguably misleadingly) entitled: 'Behind the Mask: Anonymous in the *Unauthorised Biography of Ezra Maas*.' Simons never actually lifts the mask behind which she purports to see.

The effect this figure produces on the reader is ambivalent: on the one hand Anonymous is empty. Anonymous does not have any known characteristics or (physical and psychological) traits to which the reader can cling. At best, Anonymous's personality can be inferred from the idiosyncrasies in his/her footnotes and the fact that s/he seems to know an awful lot about James and Maas (as well as – seemingly – any topic under the sun). On the other hand, Anonymous haunts you. Anonymous is the ultimate embodiment of the question that has no answer. The best way to attract attention is pretend you don't. I have heard many readers ask '*Who* is "Anonymous"?' Well, my main concern is not so much who s/he is, but rather what his/her presence means as far as authorship is concerned (Simons 140).

Simons analysis of the character of Anonymous heavily relies on her suspicion that 'we are witnessing what Derrida calls *différance*, although instead of a différance of meaning, we witness a différance of identity and authorship' (142).

Simons makes an important point here. As readers, we are constantly reminded by an anonymous voice that James heavily romanticizes the passages about his life. It is, therefore, not a question of whether James is reliable. The short answer is: he is not. What really matters once this has been established is *the extent to which* he is. The reframing of the story by Anonymous constantly brings that question to the fore, fostering a continuous sense of instability. Furthermore, Anonymous functions as a guide for the reader because they occupy the privileged space of the paratext – what Gérard Genette called the *seuil* – a space that allows them to be involved with both James and the reader, treading the fine line between fiction and reality. It is also crucial to highlight that Anonymous is not (only) James's messenger. They also expand the mirror effect between James and Maas discussed in the previous sections. In a lengthy footnote, Anonymous recounts:

> There was a time when Daniel and I were closer
> than brothers. He was my shadow and I was his.
> We may have been two people but we were one mind.
> Daniel was an extension of my true self and when
> we were alone it wasn't as if we were spending time
> with another person; it was like looking in the
> *mirror* [...] [emphasis added] (James 92-3).

Note the use of the word 'mirror' by Anonymous in order to refer to his relationship with James. The idea of 'brother-hood' and of being 'one mind' also echoes the relationship that Maas and his brother had before he passed away. The rest of the footnote further supports the turning upside down of the narrative, as Anonmyous states: '[S]omething told me that these tattered remnants were all that was left of his work the book that I had heard whispers of for years, amongst his friends and followers, his masterpiece' (93). In this case, Anonymous clearly describes James and his novel in a similar fashion as Ezra and his final artwork have been described throughout the book (using such strongly connoted terms as 'masterpiece' and 'followers'). Even the lack of reliable sources to back up James's story is reminiscent of Maas's elusive life: 'In fact there was nothing in the public domain to support his story' (Ibid.). Anonymous seems aware of that uncanny *retournement de situation*: 'I found myself in the strange position of becoming the biographer's biographer, retracing the footsteps of my former friend – my unfamiliar twin' (Ibid.). Again, he uses a vocabulary used to describe Maas and his brother's relationship. What it suggests as far the mirror effect is concerned in that James is Anonymous's equivalent of Maas. This statement is based on the metaphysical nature of James' novel, and is not incompatible with Anonymous's other possible identities. My personal guess is that Anonymous is actually ████████████████ ███████████████████████████████.[76]

IN LIEU OF A CONCLUSION: THE MAN IN THE MIRROR

For I do not exist. There exist but
the thousands of mirrors that reflect me.
– Nabokov

As the title of this essay suggests, Ezra Maas is the man in the mirror, meant in the Magrittean sense of the term. In 1937, Belgian surrealist painter René Magritte painted 'La reproduction interdite' ('Not to Be Reproduced'). It repres-

---

[76.] This part was redacted by the author herself. The publisher was unable to clarify why. As we enquired further about her involvement in this collection, it has been suggested by several different sources that she is not – in fact – who she initially purported to be. We believe that she ████████████████████████████ ████████████. We would like to subsequently apologize to the reader for the confusion – the Editor.

ents a man looking in a mirror, not at his own face, but at his back, as the reflection faces the same direction as the protagonist. His face – and therefore his identity – is bound to remain unknown. Francine Dupérêt argues: 'En peignant le reflet de dos, Magritte *frustre*. Il vole au spectateur l'occasion d'une résolution facile. A la place, une question subsiste: qui est cet homme ? Elle-même en appelant une seconde: pourquoi nous échappe-t-il ?' (Dupérêt 188).[77] 'La reproduction interdite' emphasizes the difficulty to face oneself, and the possibility to endlessly chase oneself instead. Ezra Maas escapes the protagonist's gaze, and both escape ours. And as we watch, we escape that of the spectator.

One should not, however, overlook another, more subtle, aspect of the painting which echoes James's endeavor: the presence of the novel the *Narrative of Arthur Gordon Pym of Nantucket* by Edgar Allan Poe (1838) on the mantelpiece. The last chapter of the novel recounts Pym's discovery of a labyrinth and ends abruptly when a note by the editors suggests that he died in an accident after encountering a mysterious shadow-figure. They further state that the last few chapters were lost when he disappeared: 'It is feared that the few remaining chapters which were to have completed his narrative, and which were retained by him [...] have been irrecoverably lost through the accident by which he perished himself' (Poe 179). The book in Magritte's painting is, in

---

[77.] 'By painting the reflection with its back to us, Magritte frustrates. He robs the spectator from an easy resolution. Instead, a question remains: who is that man? It even prompts a second one: why is he escaping our gaze?' (my translation).

many ways, related to the *Unauthorised Biography*, as James too disappeared along with parts of his manuscript upon allegedly meeting a shadow-being. Indeed, towards the end of the novel, James is trapped in a kind of parallel and metaphysical realm. There, he eventually meets Ezra Maas, or so he thinks:

> I spun around and saw a man with a gun standing in the middle of the road, looking back at me. It was him. Ezra Maas stood before me, at last. My own gun was still in my hand. We drew at the same time, two gunfighters facing each other at the end of the world, but only a single shot rang out. The bullet caused a crack to form in thin air. It grew larger until everything began to shatter [...] like the whole world was made of one large glass surface with nothing behind. I pulled the trigger again and again, but the figure looking back at me stood motionless. Two reflections becoming one, divided into shards, shattering into fragments, the sound of each piece of glass made as it hit the ground was the music of infinity. I realised I was looking at a mirror of the world in the middle of the road, nothing more, and when it finally fell apart, collapsing with a great crash, I saw there was nothing and no-one behind it (James 385).

This lengthy quote prompts me to go back to Dupérêt's questions regarding the meaning of Magritte's painting. Although she raises essential points, she fails to address one important question: *what* would happen if the reflection turned around? Would it be too unbearable, too complicated, too scary to even imagine? Would what we usually take for granted – a mere reflection of our self – take another dimension now that we have come back from the other side of the mirror, now that we have discovered that – after facing our self in the loneliness of a reflection – there was no one behind it? Now that we have discovered that there is *nothing*?

But after all, isn't *nothing* more real than nothing?[78]

[78.] I shall conclude this essay by a last thought. I was asked to write it by a man who refused to disclose his identity, only signing his emails with an 'X'. He told me that he had 'been approached by someone' interested in James's work on Ezra Maas.

'X,' the unknown variable, the spanner in the works.

The disruption, the question without answer.

The absence.

The absolute *nothingness*.

I am now left to wonder what my role is in the perfect machinery surrounding the work of Daniel James. Who am I supposed to be in this scheme that seems to expand beyond anything the human mind can possibly fathom?

'Capgras' delusion.' The Free Dictionary. medical-diction-ary.thefreedictionary.com/Capgras+delusion [accessed 5 Oct. 2020].

'Chiaroscuro.' The National Gallery. nationalgallery.org.uk/paintings/glossary/chiaroscuro [accessed 5 Oct. 2020].

'Doppelganger.' Literary Devices Definition and Examples of Literary Terms. literarydevices.net/doppelganger [accessed 25 Jul. 2020].

Dupérêt, Francine. 'Magritte et l'identité: l'invention de la solitude.' *Journal des Beaux-Arts de Belgique*, vol. 67, no. 2, 2012, pp. 180–189.

Grüber, Dan. 'Doppelängers and the Ghost of Goethe.' *Journal of Psychoanalysis*, vol. 18, no. 4, 2005, pp. 16–28.

Harrington, Jenna. 'Ezra Maas's Debut Novel Is Not What You Expect nor Is It What You Want.' *Forbes*, 19 Jan. 1988, pp. 12–13.

Hofstadter, Douglas. *I Am a Strange Loop*. Basic Books, 2007.

Horowitz, Ruth. 'The Nine Lives of Ezra Maas.' *Facts and Fiction*, vol. 6, no. 4, 24th Jul. 2019, pp. 23–44.

Howard, Jim. 'We Have It All Wrong.' *My Theory, a Jim Howard Journal*, vol. 1, no. 1, 29 Feb. 1974, pp. 42–49.

James, Daniel. *The Unauthorised Biography of Ezra Maas*. Dead Ink, 2022.

███████████████. 'Interview with Michelle Duncan-Horowitz.' *Time Magazine*, vol. 193, no. 2, 2019, pp. 7–9.

———

Is any of this true?

Loughlin, Jeremiah. 'The Fact That You Can Doesn't Mean You Should: This Biography Has Good Reasons Not to Be Authorized!' *L'art pour l'art*, 29 Feb. 2018, lartpour-lart.uk/the-fact-that-you-can-doesnt-mean-you-should/this-biography [accessed 21 Apr. 2022].

Moretti, Paola. 'The Fine Arts of Ezra Maas.' *The New Art Journal*, vol. 6, no. 1, 2007, pp. 12–24.

O'Sullivan, Vera. 'Game of Shadows: Ezra vs. Daniel.' *Literature and Metaphysics*, vol. 2, no. 1, 2019. pp. 20–28.

Petrakis, Maëva. 'Freud and Carroll, the Uncanny and the Mirror.' *Greek Journal of Psychology*, vol. 18, no. 4, 2001, pp. 29–43.

Poe, Edgar A. *The Narrative of Arthur Gordon Pym of Nantucket*. Harper & Brothers, 1838.

Rochas, Meryll. 'I *Still* Am a Strange Loop.' *Douglas Hofstadter's Eternal Golden Braid*. 8 Apr. 2018, douglashofs-daterseternalgoldenbraid.com [accessed 5 Oct. 2020].

Schreiber, Herman. '"The Lie through Which We Tell the Truth": Predestination and Filiations in the *Unauthorised Biography of Ezra Maas*.' *Arts and Literature*, vol. 54, no. 4, 2019, pp. 59–79.

--. 'The Not-So-Strange Loop: a Response to Douglas Hofstadter.' *Paradox and Metaphysics*, vol. 1, no. 2, 2018, pp. 9–11.

Simons, Jill. *Getting Away with Anonymity: a Study of the Trope in Contemporary Noir Literature*. Oxford University Press, 2019.

Suárez, Francesca. *The Paradox of the Suspension of Disbelief, or the Reader's Willingness to Be Fooled*. Routledge, 2004.

Am I even real?

'Suspend of Disbelief.' English Oxford Living Dictionaries. web.archive.org/web/20180729045913/https://en.ox-forddictionaries.com/definition/suspend_disbelief [accessed 30 Jul. 2020].

Vardoulakis, Dimitri. 'The Return of Negation: The Doppelgänger in Freud's "The 'Uncanny'".' *SubStance*, vol. 35, no. 2, issue 110, 2006, pp. 100–116.

--. *The Doppelganger: Literature's Philosophy.* Fordham University Press, 2010.

Are you?

A Reflection of a Reflection of a Reflection: The Danger of Truth in a Post-Truth World

John Palmer

In a world filled with fake news, fake reviews, conspiracy theories, social media bots, catfish, and troll farms, one must repeatedly ask, is this true? Increasingly often, the answer is no. In the post-truth era, *The Unauthorised Biography of Ezra Maas* hits a nerve because this postmodern novel speaks to a number of challenges and phenomena faced by individuals in the current period. As Charles Cullum notes, 'in post-modern fiction, paranoia and obsession can play positive roles in helping characters acclimate to, and even develop and maintain identity in, a chaotic postmodern world' (Cullum 2). However, when paranoia and obsession are utilized in a post-truth world, the consequences, as they are for Daniel, can be disastrous. Daniel's hunt for Ezra Maas is a defence-mechanism designed to protect his sense of identity, but due to the nature of truth in a post-truth world, this ends up being the direct cause of his self-erasure. Daniel slides so far into a world of conspiracy and fantasy, that he becomes merely a reflection of post-truth itself. This essay will examine what constitutes a post-truth world, how a post-truth world is created through the framing of the editor, and how Daniel is affected by this self-perpetuating post-truth world.

The Unauthorised Biography of Ezra Maas is a poignant reflection of the post-truth era in which a number of societies, including Britain, now inhabit. To explore this reflection, an understanding of the post-truth era must first be established. In 2016, Oxford Dictionaries announced post-truth as their US word of the year. The definition given in this announcement is as follows: 'relating to or denoting circumstances in which objective facts are less influential in shaping public opinion than appeals to emotion and personal belief' (Oxford Languages). This means that the post-truth era is built upon personal belief systems as opposed to quantifiable facts. Stephan Lewandowsky, Ullrich K. H. Ecker, and John Cook expand on this understanding of post-truth to posit that 'an obvious hallmark of a post-truth world is that it empowers people to choose their own reality, where facts and objective evidence are trumped by existing beliefs and prejudices' (Lewandowsky, Ecker and Cook 361). Due to this, personal ideologies are the defining factor as to whether or not a piece of information is true in the post-truth era.

However, post-truth does not exist on its own, it is a by-product of misinformation, disinformation, paranoia, and conspiratorial thinking. Misinformation and disinformation are two of the key factors in the creation of a post-truth world, and they are the foundations upon which this novel is built. Misinformation involves the dissemination of inaccurate information, and disinformation is a subset of misinformation that involves the purposeful manipulation of the intended audience through false information. Lewandowsky et al. argue 'that the presence of misinformation causes people to stop believing in facts altogether' (Lewandowsky et al. 355). This is due to a growing mistrust and suspicion towards the presented information. This analysis is corroborated by Don Fallis, who writes that 'disinformation can harm people indirectly by eroding trust and thereby inhibiting our ability to effectively share information with one another' (Fallis 402). Therefore, disinformation not only manipulates its intended audience, but its mere presence can sow paranoia and doubt into the minds of those that see it.

Disinformation is endemic in the UK. One example of this comes from the *Wellingborough Conservative Newsletter*, which outlines Donald Trump's weaponization of fake news, to express how Conservative Party politicians can use similar tactics to manipulate potential voters in order to win debates and elections. On page six of the newsletter, it is stated that 'if you make enough dubious claims, fast enough, honest speakers are overwhelmed' (Wellingborough Conservative News 6). Whilst page seven states 'sometimes, it is better to give the WRONG answer at the RIGHT time, than the RIGHT answer at the WRONG time' (Wellingborough Conservative News 7). This example demonstrates how a leading political party actively engages in disinformation. Lewandowsky et al. argue that in the post-truth era, 'lying is not only accepted, it is rewarded. Falsifying reality is no longer about changing people's beliefs, it is about asserting power' (Lewandowsky et al. 361). This is corroborated by Sergio Sismondo, who explains that post-truth political discourse allows for the treatment of 'voters as people to be manipulated rather than as people to be convinced' (Sismondo 4). Due to this shift into post-truth, disinformation is weaponized for personal gain.

Disseminating disinformation in this manner indirectly encourages the public's distrust in the establishment (Fallis 402). The long-term effect of being subjected to disinformation can be seen by the global report conducted for the

2021 Edelmen Trust Barometer, which states that the media is 'distrusted in thirteen countries' out of the twenty-seven that were surveyed, and that only 37% of people surveyed in the UK currently trust the media (Edelmen 45). The UK is in the midst of a post-truth crisis where paranoia is spreading and emotionally driven decisions run rampant, and *The Unauthorised Biography of Ezra Maas* is a reflection of this post-truth crisis.

The unnamed editor, whose narrative voice appears in the forward, footnotes, and afterward, frames the novel as a post-truth text. When Daniel is introduced, the truth of his account is directly brought into question by the editor in the footnotes: 'It is impossible to discount the possibility that some of what you are about to read may contain fiction' (James 8). This draws attention to the unreliability of the character, which in turn sows doubt into the mind of the reader. By doing this, the editor is able to generate suspicion which forces the reader to question the information presented in the text, as they would with the information presented in a post-truth world. Nevertheless, what truly solidifies this text as a reflection of the post-truth era appears in the afterward, which is also written by the editor: 'At the very end, this was Daniel's final gift to us; the freedom to interpret these pages as we choose' (James 391). This acknowledgement of the critical theory surrounding the Death of the Author brings the concept to the attention of the reader, and allows the editor to remind the reader of the post-truth eras primary function, which is the ability to decide what one believes based on their own personal intuition.

The novel offers a range of disinformation, from fake news articles, such as the one supposedly published by *The Guardian* online on page three, to personal statements written in the chapters titled, 'Ezra Maas: An Oral History' (James 77). This information is presented as factual, and often in a format designed to build trust, when in actuality, it is false information designed to mislead. Not only does the editor position this novel as a post-truth text, but they address the reader directly, which indicates that the reader is the actual target of the novel's disinformation: 'Yes, I have lied to you, but if I had told you the truth from the beginning, you might not have continued to read, and I couldn't risk that' (James 391). The editor, who has revealed themself to be unreliable, acknowledges their act of manipulation and presents a reason for it. However, the unreliable nature of this reasoning brings into focus the purpose of the disinformation, and as Fallis explains: 'misleading people can be (and usually will be) just an intermediate step toward a further end' (Fallis 414). This further end is arguably the editor's narrative control over the post-truth world of the novel.

The editor serves the purpose of framing the novel as a post-truth text through their narration, but they also actively construct a post-truth world by participating in a disinformation campaign and highlighting the false truths presented by Daniel:

> It is unlikely Daniel's research was incorrect as
> he was notoriously thorough, but it does raise the
> possibility that some of the people he interviewed
> about this period were either lying to him or
> giving him false information (James 127).

This functions to increase the paranoia of the reader and generate the symptoms of a post-truth world. Whilst in the afterward, the editor actively encourages the reader to choose their own reality in terms of the novel's world. Both of these actions indicate that the editor is a self-aware representation of the post-truth era, who demands a reflection be made between the world of the novel, and the post-truth world in which the reader may inhabit.

Much in the same way that the editor is a reflection of how a post-truth world functions, the character of Daniel is a reflection of an individual living in a post-truth world. When Daniel is introduced, the editor indicates the unreliability of his narrative voice, indicating that the reality he presents is one of his own creation. This is further reinforced later in the novel when the editor notes, 'Daniel was an expert in noir fiction…knowingly employing classic motifs to explore the "slippage" between reality and fantasy' (James 179). However, this indication of his unreliability is not enough to draw a parallel between him and a specific type of individual living in the post-truth era. For that to be achieved, his embracement of disinformation, his ideology, and his thought process must be analysed.

The reality Daniel chooses to present to the reader is filled with paranoia and doubt, which is to be expected in a post-truth world: 'For all the people I had interviewed and all the locations I had visited, what did I really know with any certainty?' (James 139–140). However, Daniel's willingness to embrace conspiracy, which is a form of disinformation, hints at something more insidious. Daniel's journey is a representation of the burgeoning conspiratorial thought process that has been given room to grow in a post-truth world. According to a YouGov poll conducted by Oxford University as a part of their Conspiracy and Democracy project funded by the Leverhulme Trust, 'Britain expressed a relatively strong 40% rejection of all [conspiracy] theories' (de Waal). This means that 60% of the people surveyed in 2018 believed in at least one conspiracy theory. Daniel's paranoia, and his belief in conspiracy and fantasy grows so large that he is eventually engulfed by it and unable to tell reality from fiction: 'Did I invent Maas? Or did he create me?' (James 389). His journey is a reflection of the gradual slide away from reality that individuals living in a post-truth world are at risk of making.

Michael J. Wood, Karen M. Douglas, and Robbie M. Sutton argue that a belief in conspiracy theories relies on a monological belief system grounded in a conspiratorial ideology. They argue that a monological belief system dictates that the 'incompatibilities between beliefs at a local level are dwarfed by coherence with broader beliefs about the world' because the belief itself is more important to the individual than any contradictory evidence that may prove it wrong (Wood et al. 771). How this belief affects an individual depends on their ideology: 'just as an orthodox Marxist might interpret major world events as arising inevitably from the forces of history, a conspiracist would see the same events as carefully orchestrated steps in a plot for global domination' (Wood et al. 771). This analysis is supported by J. H. Kuklinski, P. J. Quirk, J. Jerit, D. Schwieder, and R. F. Richindicates who state that when an individual is not offered all of the facts, or they are difficult to comprehend, the individual will form their own beliefs, and 'these beliefs will be inextricably intertwined with people's preferences and thus systematically biased in the direction of those preferences' (Kuklinski, Quirk, Schwieder and Rich 794). These factors combined indicate that Daniel's thought process exists in parallel to that of a conspiracist's monological belief system.

The conspiracy that Daniel chooses to engage with is that of Ezra Maas. A framework is laid out in the work of J. Eric

Oliver and Thomas J. Wood that can be used to deconstruct conspiracy theories, and it is evident that by using this method of deconstruction on Daniel's belief in Ezra Maas, that Daniel's belief mirrors a conspiracists belief in a conspiracy. Oliver and Wood argue that the majority of conspiracies have three common traits:

> First, they locate the source of unusual social and political phenomena in unseen, intentional, and malevolent forces. Second, they typically interpret political events in terms of a Manichean struggle between good and evil…Finally, most conspiracy theories suggest that mainstream accounts of political events are a ruse or an attempt to distract the public from a hidden source of power (Oliver and Wood 953).

Daniel exists inside a post-truth world, and he shifts the blame of his heightened paranoia from its sociological cause, onto Ezra Maas and the Maas Foundation, which demonstrates the first trait. For the second and third traits, it must be noted that even though the conspiracy surrounding Maas is not a political conspiracy of governmental proportions, reflections of these traits can still be drawn. The second trait becomes evident when Daniel eventually discovers Maas's true intention, it becomes apparent that Maas is one side of a Manichean struggle, and that Daniel is on the other: 'Maas had to destroy us in order to start again. He had started with me. In his eyes, the first step towards sanity was madness… The world was next' (James 370). The third trait is witnessed through the Maas Foundation's widespread disinformation campaign designed to hide Maas along with his true intentions. Through this deconstruction, it is clear that the conspiracy surrounding Maas mirrors the three traits that are common across numerous conspiracies.

It is due to Daniel's belief in these ideas and his monological belief system, that when presented with multiple pieces of contradictory evidence, he does not dismiss them, but instead decides on their validity based primarily on his personal beliefs. In a footnote about the Maas Journals and Daniel's use of them, the editor notes that 'their validity has been questioned by several sources. Daniel verified and expanded on the information from the journals, combining it with his own research and interviews' (James 29). This fits with the monological belief system presented by Wood et al. in that Daniel's conspiratorial ideology and monological belief system allows him to take contradictory and un-evidenced information and construct a unified theory, which he presents to the reader through the chapters titled 'Ezra Maas' (James 29–).

This analysis of Daniel as a conspiracist and a victim of the post-truth world in which he inhabits is corroborated further by his own chapters, which begin with a heightened level of paranoia and fantastical thinking, but as they progress, they diverge from a factual reality into an emotionally driven fantastical reality of his own creation:

I looked around the four walls. It was a room like any other, except that it was full of holes, and behind each one there were eyes watching, mouths whispering, shadows willing me to reach the end (James 386).

This parallels the construction of a conspiracist's ideology because, as Wood et al. argue, 'new layers of conspiracy [are] being added to rationalize each new piece of disconfirming evidence' (Wood et al. 767). With each added layer, the conspiracy grows more complex, until eventually, it is so far removed from reality that Daniel loses the ability to differentiate between fact and fiction.

Daniel exists in a post-truth world and from the onset of his narration, questions the nature of his own existence, but he does not resist post-truth. Instead, he readily embraces this overarching structure and fills his world with conspiracy and fantasy. His subconscious reasoning for this also matches the reasoning behind a conspiracist's reliance on fantasy.

Daniel fears his existence is under threat, and as Daniel Jolly, Karen M. Douglas, and Robbie M. Sutton argue, conspiracies 'paradoxically bolster support for the status quo when it's legitimacy is threatened' (Jolly, Douglas and Sutton 466). Daniel's own introduction to this biography brings into question his loss of identity to the reader's interpretation, as well as the transient nature of the meaning behind his words: 'Every reader changes the story, bringing it to life and making it real, every reader plays their part, just as I have played mine' (James 12). Daniel's focus on losing his sense of self to interpretation indicates a deeper fear about losing his sense of reality in a post-truth world: 'I looked into the mirror and for the first time, I didn't trust my own face (James 12). The nature of Daniel's existence is under threat, so he has latched on to a conspiracy theory and found an 'other' to blame for his woes.

Daniel's obsession with Maas and his paranoia surrounding the Maas foundation is his attempt to defend his existence and resist the disruption of his status-quo. In order to achieve this, conspiracists with a monological belief system assign blame to a select group so that they can attribute 'problems to the negative actions of outsiders while not questioning the system itself' (Jolly et al. 467). The same approach is taken with real world conspiracies such as; David Ike's belief in a reptilian race of aliens that secretly manipulate society; QAnon's belief in a cannibalistic satanic cult of paedophile celebrities and politicians; the Flat Earth Society's belief in a NASA cover up; the belief that the European Union and immigration was the cause of Britain's problems in the build-up to Brexit, and the belief that 5G is the cause of Covid-19. As Ted Goertzal writes, 'a conspiracy gives believers someone tangible to blame for their perceived predicament, instead of blaming it on impersonal or abstract forces' (Goertz 494). Daniel acknowledges his fears but refuses to address the cause of them directly. Instead, he assigns blame to a shadowy group of individuals in the Maas Foundation that are working to cover up what he believes to be true about Ezra Maas.

This reality he chooses to inhabit develops to the point that he loses himself entirely in the post-truth world, which ironically, is his initial existential fear. This becomes realised in a conversation with a voice that is arguably his own:

> *I am the voice you have heard your whole life.*
> *You have lived between fact and fiction, always*
> *wondering what was real and what was not, always*
> *wondering if your thoughts, your actions, were truly*
> *your own, always questioning the world, yourself,*
> *everything. Now you know the truth* (James 377).

The conversation ends when Daniel is told, '*you were just a reflection*' (James 378). The invention of Maas and the pursuant struggle with the truth functions as a tool to avoid questioning the limitations of the post-truth world Daniel inhabits. Daniel's monological belief system and conspiratorial ideology forces him to position the blame of his woes onto the nefarious cabal known as the Maas Foundation, whom he believes are orchestrating a conspiracy surrounding Ezra Maas. Daniel pinpoints the Maas Foundation and Ezra Maas as the cause of his problems to avoid addressing the abstract societal issues caused by the post-truth world he inhabits, because as Jolly et al. note, most people who believe in conspiracies 'view problems in society as inevitable and therefore need to find ways to adapt to them' (Jolly et al. 467). Daniel's adaption to, and embracement of, post-truth is the actual cause of his loss of identity, to the point that he becomes merely *a reflection...of a reflection...of a reflection* of the concept of post-truth itself (James 378).

In closing, this labyrinthian novel positions itself as a post-truth text through its use of two intertwining narratives. The editor frames the world of the novel as a post-truth world, but the editor is also the propagator of paranoia and the one who breaks the fourth wall to address the reader directly. Daniel James is the voice of an individual and represents the danger of monological belief systems in a post-truth world. When combined, these narrative voices instigate one of the primary functions of post-truth, which is the ability to decide what the truth is, based solely on personal ideology. The final reflection of the novel does not occur in the text, but with the reader, because they are offered the opportunity to use their own personal ideology to establish the true meaning of the text. The reader's personal ideology, like Daniel's, is subject to, and manipulated by, continuous exposure to the disinformation of the text, and as Fallis writes, 'inaccurate and misleading information can be extremely dangerous' (Fallis 402). Therefore, this novel offers a reflection of truth in a post-truth world, and in a post-truth world, the truth is dangerous.

Cullum, Charles. 'Rebels, Conspirators, and Parrots, Oh My!: Lacanian Paranoia and Obsession in Three Postmodern Novels.' *Critique: Studies in Contemporary Fiction*, vol. 52, issue 1, 2011, pp. 1–16.

de Waal, Joel Rodgers. 'Brexit and Trump Voters Are More Likely to Believe in Conspiracy Theories.' YouGov. yougov.co.uk/topics/international/articles-reports/2018/12/14/brexit-and-trump-voters-are-more-likely-believe-co [accessed 5 Oct. 2021].

Edelmen. 'Edelmen Trust Barometer 2021.' Edelmen. edelman.com/sites/g/files/aatuss191/files/2021-01/2021-edelman-trust-barometer.pdf [accessed 1 Oct. 2021].

Fallis, Don. 'What is Disinformation.' *Library Trends*, vol. 63, no. 3, 2015, pp. 401–426.

Goertz, Ted. 'Conspiracy Theories in Science: Conspiracy theories that target specific research can have serious consequences for public health and environmental policies.' *Science and Society*, vol. 11, no. 7, 2010, pp. 493–499.

James, Daniel. *The Unauthorised Biography of Ezra Maas*. Valley Press, 2022.

Jolly, Daniel, Karen M. Douglas, and Robbie M. Sutton. 'Blaming a Few Bad Apples to Save a Threatened Barrel: The System-Justifying function of Conspiracy Theories.' *Political Psychology*, vol. 39, no. 2, 2018, pp. 465–478.

Kuklinski, J. H., P. J. Quirk, J. Jerit, D. Schwieder, and R. F. Rich. 'Misinformation and the Currency of Democratic Citizenship.' *The Journal of Politics*, vol. 62, no. 3, 2000, pp. 790–816.

Lewandowsky, Stephen, Ullrich K. H. Ecker, and John Cook. 'Beyond Misinformation: Understanding and Coping with the "Post-Truth" Era.' *Journal of Applied Research in Memory and Cognition*, vol. 6, no. 4, 2017, pp. 353–369.

Oliver, J. Eric, and Thomas J. Wood. 'Conspiracy Theories and the Paranoid Style(s) of Mass Opinion.' *American Journal of Political Science*, vol. 58, no. 4, 2014, pp. 952–966.

'Oxford Dictionaries Word of the Year 2016', Languages. languages.oup.com/word-of-the-year/2016 [accessed 5 Oct. 2021].

Sismondo, Sergio, 'Editorial: Post-truth?', *Social Studies of Science*, vol. 47, no. 1, 2017, pp. 3–6.

'Wellingborough Conservative News: Newsletter 58'. mcusercontent.com/a3fe91df70df73b35c6d6fab0/files/a5c33245-3383-47cc-aa1e-7c28f9cca1f1/WCA_Newsletter_58.pdf [accessed 20 Sep. 2021].

Wood, Michael J., Karen M. Douglas, and Robbie M. Sutton. 'Dead and Alive: Beliefs in Contradictory Conspiracy Theories.' *Social Psychological and Personality Science*, vol. 3, no. 6, 2012, pp. 767–773.

Questions of Identity:
Would the real Ezra Maas
please stand up?

Hanna ten Doornkaat

palimpsest
/ˈpalɪm(p)sɛst/

noun

> 1. a manuscript or piece of writing material on
> which later writing has been superimposed
> on effaced earlier writing.
> 2. something reused or altered but still bearing
> visible traces of its earlier form.

> May I have your attention, please?
> Will the real ███████ ███████ please stand up?
> I repeat, will the real ███████ ███████ please stand up?
> We're gonna have a problem here?

A similar sentiment to Emimen's lyrics is expressed by
Stephens-Davidowitz in his bestselling book, *Everybody Lies*.
He claims that 'We are living in an age where truth has
become a construct of many truths. Our lives are controlled

by communication technology, we hang out with our mates on social media and …everybody lies'.

Reliable information is hard to come by not least due to a growing dependence on social media, and as a result do we even know whether we are not ourselves constructs controlled by algorithms ?

With this new understanding of the world in mind, I had a look at the invisible lines between the text of the *The Unauthorised Biography of Ezra Maas* by Daniel James and at the book's main characters. Who is the book about? There is Daniel James, the author, and there is Daniel James, the journalist who gets asked to write a biography of Ezra Maas, an artist who, so we are told, vanished and left everything to the Maas Foundation. This is where the confusion begins. Would the real Ezra Maas please stand up? The more we get on with the story, the more questions need to be answered, not only about the protagonist but also about Daniel, the author, and Daniel, the journalist investigating the story about the vanished artist.

It is never quite clear who addresses the reader. Is it the author of the book, or is it Daniel James the journalist in the story. Is what we get told real or is it fiction, or where does it all merge? And where in all this is Ezra Maas? It often feels like he is watching the whole story unfold from between the lines. We learn about the loss of a brother and family in his childhood, about his extraordinary intelligence which becomes a problem for him throughout his entire life. We also sense that those who claim to have met him are reluctant to talk about him. They seem scared to let us know what they know. The reader is told about photographs of those who met and partied with him but no one seems able to point him out in the pictures. Is there something sinister going on? Are they scared? Is this coincidence or a deliberate choice? It is a known fact that the art world has a very dark side and that vast amounts of money are paid for artworks at auctions, which has little to do with an interest in the artwork but everything with investments. So, it is questionable that Ezra Maas is really the person we are made believe. Does he even exist or is he a construct of the Maas Foundation? Since we are trying to find out the truth, let us for one moment consider another possibility:

What if Ezra Maas is or was a female artist like the main protagonist in Siri Hustvedt's novel 'The Blazing World'? Here the artist Harriet Burden 'embittered by the lack of attention paid her by the New York art world conducts an experiment by hiding her identity behind three male fronts in a series of solo exhibitions. The artist's story is put together posthumously through notebooks and second-hand testimonies, but every story is different which creates more mystery and there lies the key to success. The more mystery surrounds an artist, the more interesting they become for the movers and shakers of the art world. Therefore, we cannot be certain about anything that's said or written about the protagonist in *The Unauthorised Biography of Ezra Maas*. This then raises another question, who is Daniel James, the journalist? How much do we really know about him? Might there be a link between Daniel James and Ezra Maas, or could they even be the same person, or are both constructs? Is there a point in the book where we enter or exit real life versus the virtual?

Is the book about the Freudian idea of the id and super-ego mediated by the ego, with hidden memories and desires like the layers of some of the artworks described and illustrated in the book?

The story raises more questions than it gives answers and there is a constant turning of corners with moments where we think we are getting closer to the truth, only to suddenly find ourselves once again far removed from the truth or any closer to solving the mystery surrounding Ezra Maas. What truth are we looking for? Whose truth? And are we any wiser in the end? What do we know about Daniel James, the author, and Daniel James, the journalist, in the book? Are they not one and the same person? Is not a lot of the author's own character and life part of the book? Are they maybe one and the same, and could this be another trickery by the author who has created an identical twin of himself? There are a few instances where we seem to meet fragments of the real Daniel James, for example when he returns to his family and kids in his hometown Newcastle before vanishing again to hide behind Daniel James, the womaniser with a love for strong spirits. And yet another question, who is the author of all the blacked out comments and why is access denied here?

Who are we actually looking for? Seeing the invisible is what the author seems to invite us to do, the reading of the empty spaces between the lines. Maybe he is asking us to fill in the blanks and create our own story.

This is perhaps a good moment for self-reflection. The book says that 'every reader plays their part'. Where do I fit into this? A reflection on myself... Initially trained in sculpture, the underlying concept in all my work is the creation of what I consider to be a contemporary palimpsest. While my earlier sculptural work included elements of process led installations, I have focused on the meaning and concept of drawing in recent years. Working predominantly in graphite, I am concerned with examining how boundaries can be pushed, most recently creating sculptural drawings that straddle both 2D and 3D spaces. I take a lot of my inspirations from social media, dependent on algorithms and pixelations that never reveal the whole truth but always just glimpses of a fleeting moment captured on screen.

My artworks are often built up in layers where the initial idea is concealed, or appears as fragments of something barely visible. Not unlike the multiple personalities of Daniel James' and his book on Ezra Maas, the story's mysterious artist and protagonist. I believe that the way our brains function could be compared to a computer with a vast storage capacity. The brain's data and knowledge are transferred onto prepared surfaces ready to be manipulated in any way the artist wants.

I compare my own process to palimpsests in that I create a base for my graphite drawing onto a board or other suitable media at the onset of a process of erasing and redrawing lines, grids or other marks with graphite pencil, ink or biro that is repeated as many times as I feel necessary. Very often I completely erase what was there before only to then start to peel off and reveal small fragments similar to an archeological excavation. The last layer is often another layer of densely packed graphite lines once again concealing a memory of the process.

I would like my work to be a silent contemplation that should be explored, returned to, with the viewer discovering another mark each time, maybe a slip of the pencil previously undetected.

More questions... Perhaps the book is the author's comment on a radically changed world around us where truth and untruth have merged, especially in the realm of social media where any story is just a fragment or pixel of another story and when 'shaken up' by algorithms creates a new one in an instant. We will never find out the real truth about

Ezra Maas or even Daniel James, the journalist or the book's author. They constantly open and close the curtain and access is denied, no password given. Instead of a new truth we only find more confusion. Every time we think we have come a little closer we find ourselves thrown back to where we started. Would the real Ezra Maas please stand up? The story, which is constructed in many layers just like the artworks of which only fragments are described, is a psychological gameplay. Mysteries and doubts are deliberately created to confuse and remain even as we reach the end of the story. The character of Ezra Maas is carefully de-constructed and the reader is unrelentingly distracted by endless footnotes which interrupt the flow. George Santayana's quote 'there are books in which the footnotes are more interesting than the text' springs to mind. They are an important part of the investigation, like evidence of a crime scene, to piece together what happened. It is a game of constant reveal and conceal, and in the end we are none the wiser – the real Ezra Maas does not make himself known.

The Philosophers' Stoned (Lapidation)

Marc Nash

MARX OUT OF TEN

'The philosophers have only interpreted the world, in various ways. The point, however, is to change it' thus wrote Karl Marx and further thus did a stonemason carve it on the marble plinth marking Marx's place of ever-unchangingness. But Karl my dear chap, the philosophers have comprehensively failed to interpret the world definitively, not least as you cite, through offering 'various ways'. We can't even agree on fundamental frames of reference, nor first terms such as material, ideal, reality and consciousness. The starter fires his epistemological pistol loaded with blanks and a second muted detonation quickly follows hard on its heels to signal a false start. However, for all that, one can still applaud Charlie's call to action, to develop a praxis to execute a theory of change, though in what follows below, I rather apply it to art rather than politics. And to literature in particular. Though like the philosophers, we have not nailed down any singular definition of the novel, let alone a concept of fiction and thus flounder in our art rudderlessly.

Spielverlängerung: I once had a died-in-the-wool Tory
mate, (yes not like now, with us all self-sequestrated
within the rubber-walled echo chambers of social
media) {Samuel Johnson [see below] was a Tory,
figures}, who had a reader's ticket to the old British
Library in the British Museum in Bloomsbury.
Because he knew that Karl Marx had been a frequent
reader there while he researched *Das Kapital*, my mate
figured out that if he sat in a different seat each time
he visited, he could decisively state that he had sat in
the same seat as Karl Marx. Pretty broad-minded for a
Tory I thought. But then despiteful me gleefully knew
Marx had suffered from haemorrhoids and hidradenitis
suppurativa (boils and perianal inflammation).
I suppose in his favour however, they're not infectious,
not after 170 years anyway. A bit like Marxism these
days. Now Marx's tomb has been attacked many times,
including with explosives, one of the most materially
destructive of forces, just because some people didn't
agree with his ideas. What could be more of a symbol
of man's fallacious and confused thinking, than to wage
material war on the realm of idealism? To blow up the
tomb of an already dead person. The British Library,
under the impulsion of progress and shelf-space for
ever burgeoning published titles, has moved out of the
British Museum. I don't know if my mate managed to
cover all the seat permutations with his arse cheeks or
not. I can no longer ask him, since social media
determines he and I can't be friends (Spielgefährtin)
any more.

Samuel Johnson (whilom chief lexicographic wrangler of the English language) claimed to disprove Bishop Berkley's primacy of consciousness and idealism over the material world, by kicking a stone with the imitable 'I refute it thus'. However, the contingent radiation of pain waves transmitted solely to his brain, no more proves the materiality of the stone than it does that of Samuel Johnson. Boswell who was accompanying him back from the Berkeley (historical figure, not current US university) lecture, experienced no such petrous related sensations. Another man wearing steel toe-capped boots, is far less likely to feel pain when kicking the same stone and indeed the steel may be so deadening of any sensation of the stone's counter-force, that he may not feel the materiality of the stone against it at all. While a foot-baller striking a ball, gets no such transmission of pain and indeed his muscle memory will filter out all sensation other than that perhaps of whether it was a clean strike, but cer-tainly no fanciful notions or proofs of the ball's materiality. When the same footballer strikes towards a ball but manages to miss making contact with it, there can be absolutely no messages of materiality sent to his brain. However, the boos and invective of the frustrated supporters in the stands will wreak an effect on his mind, thus further affirming the agency of subjective perception rather than materiality of which there was none at that point. Now, admittedly a leather ball scores less on any scale of density and hardness, (we'll have to employ the Wentworth rather than the Brinell, seeing as the latter is an indentation measure, which would probably puncture the ball), yet both must possess the same

level of materiality or immateriality as one another, whether
both are kicked, missed or stepped over (*lollipopped'* in the
football vernacular). The stone and the ball look different,
feel different to the touch, especially to the toes and occupy
different contexts; the football being an invention of man's,
the stone being adapted to all sorts of uses, from dry wall
erection, to ballista siege engine to take down citadel dry
walls. The rules and methods of warfare are certainly con-
jurations of human invention, as are the rules of association
football (Spielregeln).

> Spielverlängerung: Urchins, rascals and rapscallions
> of yore, would play a dastardly trick of hiding a large
> stone under a hat lying on the pavement and waiting
> for a person to come along who would kick the hat
> and get rewarded with toe throes for their pains.
> Now, which is the greater rogue, the ragamuffins for
> setting the trap, or the man with implicit violence in
> his soul who launches a kick for the aimless purpose
> of destruction to the hat? Resist giving vent to the
> seething frustrations in your breast and your tootsies
> persist unthrobbingly. These days you don't see such
> a prank played (einen Streich spielen), partly because
> there are fewer men sporting hats, save for the denizens
> of Hoxton and Shoreditch. Stones and other masonry
> however, remain available for repurposing as missiles
> during street confrontations with the police in urban
> riots. Repurposing material objects plays merry hell
> with their designated nomenclature.

In his painting 'The Treachery of Images', René Magritte has painted a pipe and the motto underneath it 'Ceci n'est pas une pipe' ('This is not a pipe'). And by Jove, that canny Belgian draughtsman's bang on the money. It isn't a pipe, it's a painting of a pipe. Or rather a painting of the symbol we recognise as a pipe. A smoking pipe that is, not a piece of duct piping that channels away rainwater from your guttering, or the sudsy scum from your tumble-drier. The treachery of language. Context is all. But there's a further layer of interpretation/meaning/sense perception: it's actually (only) dollops of paint on a canvas. The essence of its materiality. It's only our conscious minds that recognise René's carefully scraped paint stylings, to have a patterned form that we construe/construct as a smoker's pipe. And then he only goes and denies us that insight, the contrarian. But we authors and word wranglers can come right back at him with the zinger, (idiomatic term for a 'burn' or 'dis', not the burger option on a KFC™ menu), 'hey Magritte, stay in your own lane; your waggish painting wouldn't work without the words', where words should have no place in visual art. The only thing an author has on their palette are words. 'Je ne Magritte rien' he might reply waggishly. Authors cannot describe the materiality of anything when they only have words to do so. They may well spark images and pictures inside a reader's imagination, but they do not actually exist. 'This is not a Victorian parlour and these characters are not really playing a parlour game' (Gesellschaftsspiel) would be the motto on the picture conjured up by the power of Jane Austen's descriptive writing. Ergo fiction writing (and all writing too for that matter), cannot reproduce realism (assuming the real even exists), since the only materiality it bears is printer's ink on paper. Flimsy.

Spielverlängerung: Abstract Expressionist painting by the likes of Pollock and Rothko bear out the fundamentalism of the third layer of interpretation of 'The Treachery Of Images', because having stripped out the figurative, they only offer colour, light and texture of the paint layers to the eye. All art can tell us, is about art. All fiction can tell us about, is fiction. *The Unauthorised Biography of Ezra Maas* confoundingly tells us about art AND fiction in one text, but does have the good grace to not dance around their ambages. At the precise moment of having become becalmed in art (and probably literature too), as we enter its period of début de siecle decadence, maybe we have at long last reached the point of understanding this fundamental first principle.
However, that does not stop the gallery viewer seeing in Rothko's canvases the fires of Hell, the ovens of Auschwitz (glass half empty), or the kinetic energy trails of angels or matter itself (glass half-full, actually, define your terms, what do you mean by i glass ii full/ empty?). Even if there is nothing but the essentialism of matter on show, the human mind will strive mightily to detect pattern in it and from that to delineate symbol. Pattern? Symbol? As an author I appeal to the stone and refute them thus. Mankind is incontestably drawn to finding pattern wherever (s)he can. Perhaps (s)he is hard-wired to do so. Pattern provides predictability for the senses,

which helps the calculating brain make its decisions. Chaos and disorder in the data of our senses, would make such calculations far harder, if not impossible. Aesthetically we appreciate symmetry in architecture, euphonious harmony in music. But the external world, if it exists objectively outside our individual subjectivities, is not necessarily symmetrical, harmonious or patterned. Yet our pattern-ravening minds impose just such schemata on it. Physicists laud the elegance of the simple equation to explain the physical world (never mind that such equations fall short at the planetary and sub-atomic levels). We are drawn to aesthetically pleasing animals in Nature and repulsed by the disordered-looking 'ugly' ones. Yet all fauna are asymmetrical when properly observed, it's what gives human beings their individuality on a physical level. Our sense perception works on the scale we operate in, 5-6ft tall upright, eyes frontal not on the side with attendant blindspots, perceiving in three dimensions. Yet current theories of Physics posit existence in ten(+?)-dimensions, so where does that leave our paltry sense perception abilities? Things look symmetrical or aesthetic to us in three dimensions, but that doesn't mean they are inherently so in higher dimensions. Art has nailed its colours to the mast emblem of pattern. Therefore at best it reproduces the little illusions and delusions we rely on to make the physical world comprehensible. (Even within Abstract Expressionism, while Rothko and Pollock offer no significant meaning in their arrangements, Mondrian pursued geometric pattern based on his observations of New York). Literature under the stranglehold of

Aristotelean Poetics, of organising narrative into beginning, middles and ends, is no less culpable. Another foundational reference frame we have failed to pin down is that of time and yet time is fundamental within the novel. Our lives do not proceed according to beginnings, middles and end, since we are without awareness right at the beginning at birth, while we have no end until we die; rather we just live our lives consecutively, not in ordered narrative episodes like fictional characters do. We are not actors (die Schauspieler) in our own lives, playing out scenes. If we have motivations, we are only dimly aware of some of them and rather than flashbacks, we are stuck (ulp, suck it up) in repetitive patterns of behaviour. That's why psychotherapy is still a thing. Worth noting that Pollock fatally stacked his car into an object that demonstrated its materiality by proving an immovable force and Rothko lethally slashed his wrists. Both were thanatotic heavy drinkers. Sour grapes from Rothko and Pollock stock and barrel. I'd say both were glass half-empty merchants, except as dipsomaniacs, their glasses were more often than not probably fully empty.

GOD ONLY KNOWS

God, wait what now, we're treating god as a philosopher? Sure, well why not? He left us texts, little coded clues along his Gematria treasure hunt towards salvation/enlightenment/ redemption, for his interpreters, scholastics and exegesists to follow like a divine Pokémon GO™. So divine we must. But fret not, we invoke a couple of bona fide philosophers later. God was the great, original creator (Spielgestalter) 'In the beginning was the logos and the logos was with God' (John 1:1). Now 'logos' is a word with a complexity of meaning. As an unchanging truth of existence, it is often just simplified to 'The Word'. In the beginning was the word and the word was with god. Before he created Adam, God pulled his finger out and at its tip created the physical universe and named everything. He was in possession of the power of both verbs and nouns. However, once Adam came along, God graciously split his power, 'So he took some soil from the ground and formed all the animals and all the birds. Then he brought them to the man to see what he would name them; and that is how they all got their names' (Gen 2:19). God still disincarnatedly embodied the verbs, but now mankind got the naming rights of His products. But with the Fall, there is another switch,

'Because of what you have done, the ground will be under a curse. You will have to work hard all your life to make it produce enough food for you' (Gen 3:19). So verbs are now a punishment and the burden of man. However, we still retained the power of naming things. Grouping and classifying things by shared taxonomic features, by replicated pattern. And boy have we made a pig's ear of it. Pattern you see, delivers us into evil problems every time. Many nouns betray their pictographic roots: the hippocampus of the brain, named after a supposed resemblance to the sea horse, itself a same-shaped long face as the horse, so literalised as a (miniature) horse that lives in the sea. The amygdala named after the Latin for almond, of which it again figuratively resembled. Thus many nouns are already their own metaphors, symbols embodied in their etymology. So to pen a metaphor is like a double exposure. An over-egging of the pudding, if you can forgive the metaphor (I can't). If words did their job with requisite precision, without the slippage and leeway (Spielraum) we wouldn't need metaphor. Words can't describe or even construct reality, anymore than figurative or landscape art can. Or heaven forfend, a camera. But at least such visual art forms announce their limitations by their output only being in two dimensions (saving sculpture). Words are without dimensionality at all. Else they possess mutable dimensions, dependent on the imagination of the author and their readers. Conceive an author describing their narrator walking through a city. Either the sights are left unremarked upon and just form a list, or the narrator applies emotional and/or symbolic resonance to what some of these sights mean for them. The first {litotes} is pointless, because a list of words cannot describe reality (merely adumbrate it); the second {hyperbole} is utterly subjective, since the sight of a pram missing a wheel is going to mean something to a recently bereaved mother and something different to a rioter looking for something to transport broken masonry proto-missiles to his comrades confronting the cops. Fiction by definition is a product of the imagination, therefore it can't be reality can it?

Spielverlängerung: Phenomenology as produced by the likes of Husserl, return us to the Berkeley V Johnson divide, I think therefore I am, versus I stub my toe therefore the stone is. Phenomenologists try to be all things to both men, hard up stubbed toes while also admitting that the painful proof thereof, is constructed within the subjective mind. Any object that is close enough to hand so as capable of being picked up or touched, is proof enough of its material substance. (And the ancient measurement of a cubit was determined by the length of a man's forearm, so there is the similar problem of the diversity of human anatomical dimensions; if a child cannot reach the fruit bowl to help himself, does the apple not exist?). Wittgenstein took a similar position when he said that the pursuit of human knowledge should only concern itself with useful things that formed part of our lives (and thereby putting himself out of a job, since philosophy itself didn't to his mind comply with such measure of utility). But the phenomenologists fall foul of the nominalism bequeathed to Adam and near synchronously explored by Plato in his ideal forms. The ideal form of any object, which for Plato could not exist in the material world of poor copies and imitations, bears a striking resemblance to the word for it, as part of the logos; it is flawless, unchanging and eternal. Nominalism out-trumps phenomenology before it's even got off the launch-pad. A stone is only one of many unrelated objects that if you kick at it, will hurt your toe. They are first differentiated by being named and classified, a stone, a wall, a car, a landmine etc. Its name and also its verbally conferred group attestation, precede any proof of its substantiality by kicking it, or skimming it across water, or throwing it at a policeman's tithead helmet, or building a dry wall or a Japanese rock garden out of it. The key context for the stone, being provided here by the verb, the doing or action word involving the stone's fate. Everything comes back to language and naming things, which puts novelists back on top potentially, though of course most don't even dare try and wrangle what they ought to be wrangling, with regard to language and reality's artificially convenient construct. If the Abstract Expressionists finally attained art's foundation stone, then authors really ought to be doing similar for their own artistic medium and that is deal with, and in, language. From that can stem all the notions about reality, perception, consciousness, being and existence that it currently claims to offer 'truths' upon, but falls so far short that it offers very little of use to us and our experience. Fiction is a playground (Spielplatz) and language its plaything (Spielzeug). Time to get serious.

Spielerweiterung: *The Unauthorised Biography of Ezra Maas* is a quantum shadow play (Schattenspiel) of a {visual} artist seeking to erase himself and an investigative journalist (who may or may not be the 'real' author Daniel James) who is seeking to construct him through documentary 'proofs' and verbal attestations, in order to attain the artist's material body. I commend it to you as your freies Spiel. Bereit Spieler eins?

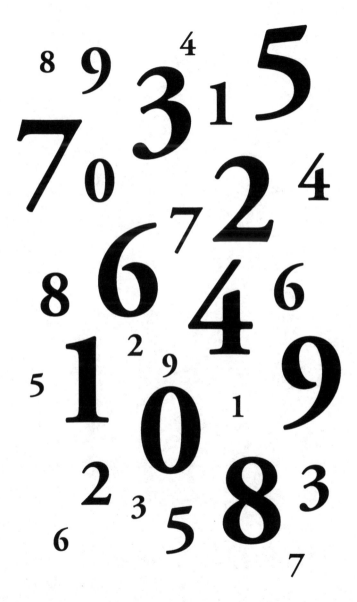

What do the numbers mean?

More Than Just Another Book

Ted Curtis

Life wasn't linear, and if my book hoped to tell the truth it couldn't be either... you start to lose a sense of where and when... it was a kind of possession.

The Unauthorised Biography of Ezra Maas is quite a read, one so multi-layered as to defy attempts at categorisation from all angles, or any delimiting terms such as modernist, post-modern, metafiction, biography or gumshoe noir. Daniel James successfully manages to mix the last three or four of these with biography and a crash course in art and architectural history, literature, and philosophy, whilst placing a fictionalised version of himself at dead centre: all in all, it's no mean feat. I thought at first the relentless footnotes would put me off, as they often do with David Foster Wallace, but after a short time their effect was to provide further immersion in the world of *The Unauthorised Biography of Ezra Maas*, implicating the reader thoroughly in the protagonist's doomed venture and the dark mystery at the heart of it – at first you feel like you're drowning in them, but before too long, it's as if you need them in order to stay afloat. This is even true of the ostensibly irritating ones, the ones that tell you just where a European beer is from and exactly how it's brewed, or how wild garlic is harvested in the Basque region of Spain for the purposes of local rustic cuisine, or even who Fluxus were. About three quarters of the way through *The Unauthorised Biography of Ezra Maas*, James goes full-on postmodern with a two-page footnote explaining the purpose of all the (500+) footnotes. That's me kind of sailing close to giving too much away, but as it's nothing to do with the plot as such, I don't consider this to be a spoiler.

The book's structure is, on a basic level, a documentarian one, like the packages-as-chapters concept employed by Peter Carey in *A True History of the Kelly Gang* taken many steps further, and those ubiquitous footnotes only serve to embellish and reinforce this. The narrative sections are the chapters from James's book-within-a-book, and these are broken up by transcripts of telephone conversations and podcasts, recorded notes made on a smartphone, letters from the authorities concerning the protocol of how you would go about declaring a person dead absent a body, magazine pieces, redactions, oral histories and more, all wrapped up in a classic private detective noir, one with the more than a slight air of otherness, of the supernatural – in many ways it felt a little like Alan Parker's 1987 classic modern noir movie *Angel Heart*.

The ostensible plot is that the Daniel James of the novel is contracted by an anonymous agent to write a biography of the reclusive conceptual artist and synaesthetic savant Ezra Mass, who has disappeared, supposedly to prepare his final artwork. The agent offers James an incredible, unspecified amount of money: James is in considerable debt and his career's on the skids, he's described by some as a showman and a charlatan, by the anonymous friend providing the footnotes as *a man who had always had a complicated relationship with the truth*; but there's more to his taking on the job than this. He's fascinated, and quickly becomes enmeshed, obsessed, as his mind incrementally disintegrates. The job also pits him against the sinister Maas Foundation, as well as his army of lunatic fans – notoriously litigious, the Foundation have been expunging all information on Maas from the internet since his disappearance, leaving only their own website, ezramaas.com. This gave the novel a slight *Blair Witch Project* feel, in terms of viral marketing (the website's very convincing), at least at first, and I was also reminded of Adam Nevill's *Last Days*, wherein a washed-up indie filmmaker is employed to make a documentary on an international Mansonesque apocalypse cult from the 1970s, and to uncover whatever's happened to its surviving members, But although I did enjoy *Last Days*, *The Unauthorised Biography of Ezra Maas* is a far more accomplished novel, one that will keep you thinking of it between reading sessions, and for long afterwards too, and I'm afraid Last Days seems like pulp by comparison. As Daniel careers around Europe and the United States, meeting warning after warning, encountering horror after death after portent, and more and more disturbing pieces of information about Maas's past and the origins of the Foundation, we are there with him every step of the way, holding his hand, telling him, *no Dan, don't look, take a step back, please, no more mate; can't you see what going on here*, knowing all the time that he can't. Because he has to go on, he has no choice. He's chasing, among other things, the last copy of an unnamed film Maas made, one with encoded mathematical messages that are said to drive the viewer insane and to have seizures – indeed, the first death he encounters, Jane, pleads with him via her diary/suicide note, *don't watch the film*. Rarely have I felt so thoroughly involved with and hypnotised by a novel. Because this seems like more than just another book. It will not so much draw you in as drag you to its febrile core, shaking your bones to dust and robbing you of all sleep and peace of mind as you go. Really. I mean it.

Unauthorised Social Media

Amy Lord

A good book stays with you long after you've turned the last page. But how many books can you name that extend beyond the margins, creating a presence in the real world?

Ezra Maas and his foundation came to readers' attention through Daniel James' 2018 book, but they exist beyond the pages of his unauthorised biography. Maas's reach extends online, a shadowy presence that offers a hint at life in the digital realm.

A quick search online brings up a Maas Foundation website and social media presence, the latter dating back to 2012, which provokes as many questions as it does answers. Expanding on the postmodern vision of the novel, this online profile is enough to tantalise, to take the inquisitive reader once again down the rabbit hole, proving the book's meta credentials. Is the Maas Foundation found only within the pages of the novel, or is it something more?

There's a lot to play with here and it's something fans of the book have responded to, the opportunity to immerse themselves in a mysterious subculture that contains endless stories within stories. Many have a foundation in reality, lending credence to those whose origins which are less certain.

'How far down does
the rabbit hole go?'

The Maas Foundation (@MaasFoundation) · FOLLOWS YOU
· The official representatives of visionary artist Ezra Maas
#EzraMaas · London, New York, Paris · ezramaas.com · Born
January 1 · Joined July 2012 · WE ARE FOLLOWING YOU ⋯
Paul Fulcher (@fulcherpaul) · I have spotted what I suspect
is a hidden message signalled in the footnotes to the updated
version of *The Unauthorised Biography of Ezra Maas* by (or
attributed to) @danjameswriter and bravely re-published by
@valleypress. This is a deliberate change since the previous
editions and makes me suspect there is a hidden message,
the missing footnote 146/150, encoded in the artwork on page
88. But who has the key to the code? The @MaasFoundation?
And what does it reveal? ⋯ Jeff Falzone (@jefffalzone) · For
those sneaky souls who are tracking the JD, ED, EM connections, please note the names on the plaque and the number.
Hopefully you have your copies of *The Easy Chain* and
Ezra Maas in hand. The mystery deepens. ⋯ Jason Denness
(@Felcherman) · Apr 16 · Replying to @MrsAMcCulloch ·
Well that was silly. @MaasFoundation know what you look
like now. ⋯ Stu Hennigan (@StuHennigan) · Apr 16 · Replying to @Felcherman · @MrsAMcCulloch and @Maas-
Foundation So they're following you too......? ⋯ Beyond
The Zero Podcast (@beyondzeropod) · What the actual fuck
is this black fucking helicopter doing circling my fucking
house at 4am @MaasFoundation??? ⋯ Brian Ward (@Brian-
Ward222) · Praise continues to roll in for @danjameswriter's
masterful *The Unauthorised Biography of Ezra Maas*. Only a
matter of time before the @MaasFoundation intervenes to

You have been warned.

halt the spread of this subversive work, so enjoy it while you can. #theunauthorisedbiographyofezramaas ⋯ Mookse (@mookse) · It was with great trepidation that I published a review on the site that may anger the Maas Foundation! ⋯ Olga Wojtas (@OlgaWojtas) · I remember meeting Ezra Maas in a crowded Edinburgh cafe in 2001. I was waiting for a friend, and a man asked if the seat was free. I said no and he went away. He looked about 50, which is how I know it was him. Wish I had asked for an autograph. #EzraMaas ⋯ Indie Bookshops (@IndieBookshopUK) · I love the playfulness of #EzraMaas, we had arranged to take a portrait in a playground in London and after an hour this was the closest we got to a successful shot. ⋯ Paul Fulcher (@fulcherpaul) · If #maaslives why does he have an estate? Very suspicious ⋯ *The Unauthorised Biography of Ezra Maas* by @danjameswriter – read the book and you will find your twitter account being followed by a shadowy foundation and that's just the start ⋯ Jason Denness (@Felcherman) · @MrsAMcCulloch Have you been getting spammed/stalked by @MaasFoundation? Been quiet for a while, looks like it will be kicking off in 2022. ezramaas-wiki.org #MaasLives ⋯ Alison McCulloch (@MrsAMcCulloch) · Jan 20, 2021 · Replying to @Felcherman and @Maas-Foundation · Yes I have!! Emails with links I dare not click on. All very suspicious if you ask me ⋯ Jason Denness (@Felcherman) · Jan 20, 2021 · Replying to @MrsAMcCulloch and @MaasFoundation · They are getting better at hiding the black vans, not seen one of them yet #MaasLives

#DanielJamesIsDead

A Family History, 1935–1976

Henry Eves

Dear ███████,[79]

I discovered the following incomplete manuscript
after moving house recently. It was beneath the
upstairs box-room carpet and appears to be part of
some extensive notes for a dissertation or biography
by someone called Henry Eves. Many of the pages
have been rendered unreadable due to the ongoing
damp issues in this house (*Delightfully bohemian,
shaded, mid-terrace, red brick with small backyard.
This would a great first rung leg-up for the right person.*

---

[79]. The identity of this individual has been the subject of
much speculation. However, the most likely candidate is
writer and poet Nick Reeves. We believe he should be
credited with assembling this work and presenting it to
the publisher for inclusion in this collection – *Anonymous*

In need of some TLC!). I'm sure you'll agree with me when I say that, despite being poorly written in places, it has a certain charm. As far as I can see, it appears to be the history of an ice cream business. But as the only writer I know in the local area, I thought I should pass it onto you. I also thought the family name might pique your interest given your friendship with a certain Mr James...

Sincerely,

███████████ (Mrs)

#

1910

Born during the morning of September 20th, Fiovana, Italy, to Maria and Captain Augusta-Franck Maas, the boys are named Ezra-Sylvester and Sylvester-Ezra. The unusual pairing of the names being something of a tradition in rural Italy.

1914

The family relocate to Turin where Augusta-Franck is stationed at the famous horse garrison. He is promoted to the rank of Major. This is remembered as a particularly happy period for the young family. The boys enjoy fencing & adopt the regiment dwarf pony, Fonzi. Unfortunately, their time at the garrison is short-lived as war breaks out over Europe.

1916

Major Augusta-Franck Maas [*Turin Brigade xiv*] is killed in action at Caporetto, Slovenia,[80] during an ill-fated cavalry charge against superior enemy forces. The family move back to Maria's hometown, Fiovana, in the Trussanzi mountains, where the boys learn to ski & goat herd.

1915–20

The twins attend various schools.

[*text missing*]

1928

Ezra-Sylvester applies to study Geography at Verona University but fails to sit the entry examination as he becomes lost for several days in the unfamiliar city.

> …my brother, he disappeared for a weekend in Verona.
> A weekend! Mama was frantic. Myself, I figured that
> he was chasing the skirts, the *sophisticates*, the city girls!
> Ah, who could blame him? We had tired of the rough,
> country girls. By this time Fiovana, well, let me put
> it this way, we had baked that particular ciliegia torte!
> (*cherry cake*). As it turned out, my brother was just
> hopelessly lost… (*Gelato!*)

[80.] See Dr. F.D. Felicini's excellent account of this battle: *Gorizia! – Gas! Gas!* Roma University Press, 1957.

1929

Ezra-Sylvester joins his uncle's ice cream restaurant, Franco's of Fioricci, as a dishwasher. During his time here he begins to learn the Maas ice cream recipes. His brother joins him later that winter. Franco's ice cream parlour becomes a well-known meeting place for stars of stage and screen as well as politicians. Benito Mussolini was a regular customer, visiting whenever he was in the area.'

> …Bennie, (Mussolini) for he was this to me, was a
> big fan of the almond & raspberry knickerbocker.
> He would often eat two all the while signing this
> and that document (*Gelato!* 59–61).

[*see plate 15 – Franco 'Fingers' Maas can be seen
to the left of the photograph, juggling spoons*]

[*text missing*]

FEBRUARY 1931

The Scatessio racecourse tragedy.

JUNE 1931

Following the Scatessio Valentine's Day racecourse disaster that year, which lay claim to both their mother & Uncle Franco, among many others, the twins board the SS Burundi bound for New York. However, they decide to disembark at Portslyn, England.

We had stood on the damp deck of that damn
tramp steamer, in our flannels and our red braces,
long enough. The English breeze, the countryside,
well… she just took our breath (*Gelato!* 177).

[*text missing*]

The Maas twins open their first ice cream parlour on the
outskirts of Barton Sands, Penn Beacon. 'A surprising
success!' says *The Weston Gazette* (w/e June 1933)

The success of the ice cream parlour was a surprise
to almost everyone – everyone, but Ezra-Sylvester
and myself. If we had opened it on the mainland,
in Weston or Bruchester we would, no doubt, have
attracted the interest of the higher classes, those with
the money and the time. But we were young and foolish.
And poor. We could not afford to step straight into
that society… The only properties affordable to us
we out on Penn Beacon (*Gelato!* 268–300).

[*text missing*]

– a long line of Italian creatives, the twins knew inherently
that to make a success of anything one had to take business
to the people who wanted … [*text indistinct here*] '…
even so,' she said. 'We all simply adored their ice cream …'

[*text missing*]

— reasoned (with an acumen that some later attributed to genius, recklessness, or luck — these last folk were, probably, just jealous).

> … if we could sell the cooling ices and sorbets at
> almost cost, from a cheap premises, to those with
> the driest throats… then we could make a go of it
> in this new world (*Gelato!* 259)

It is not known whether it was Ezra-Sylvester or Sylvester-Ezra who came up with the idea of selling ice cream to the quarrymen first, as no clear record exists. Some think one, some think the other.

#

Ezra-Sylvester was the eldest, by some nine minutes, and was the first of the two to be a talker (apparently). He was quiet and reflective and could be sullen. He was prone to chest infections and hallucinations as a boy. Despite these ailments he was the first of the two to be a walker (apparently): this is all merely hearsay about the young Maas boys, and there is suggestion that the attributes have been confused with the passing of time; so, who knows? The important (and clear) thing is that two young Italian boys arrived in the area in that thin spring of '33 and, one or other, both, embarked on an idea that would become a surprising success.

The Hollows, as that area of the peninsula was known locally, was home to those employed in the quarrying industry. The name itself is thought to be a reference to the intricate network of open pits that riddle this part of the county. The Hollows stretched along a particularly desolate and dreadful part of Penn Beacon. Any trees that still stand there are bent almost double and bow to the east. At the time of the Maas' arrival half acre plots could be bought for as little as £100. This was due to a number of reasons, including, obviously, the terrific scarring of the land, the constant rock face explosions, the pest problems, and the poor sanitation issues.

> – wandering semi naked one afternoon. The arresting officer found him to be both 'incoherent & confused.' His clothing was later discovered on the roof of the Eight Kings public house. One has to question –
> (*Gelato!* 300)

[*text missing*]

Five pits dominate the landscape. The Hollows was also the site of the local municipal dump. The dump dates back to Victorian times and sprawled alongside the blast area and the shanties and the blackened milk.

[*text missing*]

… skies were littered with terns. Of course, these days, this particular area is now the site of the Hollows Estate which promises 'popular traditional modern living at affordable prices' (brought to you by the Jurassic Homes Co.) – a bronze statue of a quarryman stands at the entrance to Ramsden Drive Car Park, although it is sadly in need of care and attention due to excessive guano build-up and some vandalism. [*see image*]

The front of the Maas Ice Cream Parlour ('ices, sorbets, cola') was dressed in pale blue and white and was quite incongruous among the scruffy and scant selection of dark, pokey businesses and timber dwellings in that neighbourhood. An elaborate and quite ornate etching in the plate glass of two rotund and smiling moustachioed gentlemen, tipping top hats in saluta-tion, greeted you as you approached [*see plate 25*] (*Gelato!* 280).

[*text missing*]

… the tinkle of spoons sang out against shapely glass bowls and crooked teeth.' The quarrymen gravitated to the parlour after leaving their shifts at the face and word soon got around that the delicious Italian ice cream was the perfect way to ease the grit-cake and dust-coat from their mouths.

The glistening globes of –

[*text indistinct*]

– black, also, and green, was dragged back down onto chests
or else was trumpeted out with gusty salvoes into the paper
serviettes that read Maas in swirled pale blue lettering. The
tables were bare board, busy with crushed almonds and ash
and dust, leathered elbows, and palms as big as spades.

> The lips of these filthy creatures, only that last hour
> risen out of the quarry {became} painted and glossy
> in the cutlery and glass, with the sticky raspberry sauce.
> Tongues darted and lolled, and the thick and melodic
> voices of the quarrymen rose and fell, bringing a choral
> joy to [*indistinct text due to excessive damp staining*] ...

> – It was, as has been noted, a thin spring that year
> and a handwritten sign on the door requested that
> patrons should '*please close*' it behind them on entering
> or leaving the premises. Many of the rock men,
> being illiterate, paid no heed to this request and
> quite soon the twins, bemused, took the sign down
> and supposed that these hardy types preferred to be cold.
> The customer, it is said, is always right! (*Gelato!* 444)

The twins turned tables, collecting, and delivering bowls,
chatting with the men, neat hands in apron, on hips, friendly
claps on black, broad and broken backs. By the second year
they purchased another, larger, property on the mainland
at Weston and that became as popular as the first. It was
also called Maas' and catered for families of the local busi-
nessmen. And again, it was the boys' kind and professional
attitude to business that made the twins a success among
the town folk. That, and the delicious ice-cream sundaes
and knickerbocker glories that required the longest spoons

to mine the creamy fruit and nut delights from the tall
glasses.

[*text missing*]

[*image*]

The open pit families lived in a ramshackle
slum of shacks and huts that were
scattered all along the cliff top.

[*text missing*]

– if he had just been a fraction taller, well, it would have been
a completely different story! The fireman was later presented
with a bravery medal, which, if you ask me, he most certainly
did not deserve!' (Francesca Manson would go on to serve
four years in Penn Beacon prison, all the time protesting
her innocence). It is often said that after the incident with the
steam engine Ezra-Sylvester never touched red meat again.
In fact, it is said that even the sight of deer could anger him.

[*text missing*]

– she broke her arm one evening while walking
the neighbour's Dachshund, Rory. The wind that
evening would have been easterly and the house itself,
due to extensive renovation work on the west wing,
was quite open. Dr. Clutter was duly summoned from
The Eight Kings where he was on call (*Gelato!* 578).

By the time war broke out the Maas family had a string of
ice cream parlours stretching from Barton Sands to
Dorchester in the east and Lymington in the west. They
employed some 60 locals, and the twins would be sure to
turn up and chat with the customers and always roll up
their sleeves and get stuck into the clearing of tables and, of
course, the serving of ices. By now, the larger of the Maas
parlours had moved into serving alcoholic beverages alongside the cola and lemonades and teas that accompanied the
frozen desserts. Some of the properties were large fifty seat
venues, whilst many were smaller kiosks dotted along the
coast like Roman wall watchtowers.

[*text missing*]

… somewhere along the coast at Charmouth – as
unlikely as this seems! This stroke of luck enabled
her to move to the Norfolk Broads, where she had
an old auntie who had once been a singing star in
London, but now lived on a pittance in Wrexham
with several dozen cats (*Gelato!* 589).

[*Notes On War. First draft.*]

Sylvester-Ezra enlisted and within weeks had left the county on a train to London and from there he took a steamer to France. He was never seen or heard of again.

#

Ezra-Sylvester married a Penn Beacon girl called Sylvie Trott (*b.1919 Penn Beacon. d.1969* Kreuzberg). She was willowy and blind in one eye. By July 1943, he waved both her and the town goodbye from, by some neat twist of fate, the deck of the SS Burundi. His capacity aboard the 50,000 tonner this time was as chef.

He was one of a team of six whose job it was to feed the crew of thirty-four merchant seamen. The Burundi sailed from Portslyn and from there was employed as a supply ship between America and England. People often talk about _____ (*the grey wolves…is this right?? Check this!!*), but Ezra-Sylvester claims in his biography that he was never once bothered by U-boats or bad dreams at sea. He returned in December 1944, demobbed, and went back to the ice cream business as if he had just popped outside for a _____ {*urination?? pasty?!*}

[text both indistinct & missing here]

'– business lost some of its custom after the war years. There was the ongoing debacle with J. Jackson & Jackson (solicitors) to keep in mind. By this time, E.S. Maas' opium intake had reached outrageous proportions & he ran the business from his bathtub where he would soak hour after hour, dozing & drinking gin. Ever loyal, Roy, his erstwhile lover, describes the state of affairs at the Maas house as 'Sad. Very, very sad. Very sad.' He, too, by that Christmas, would find himself out on the streets.

[text missing & unreadable
in places due to heavy staining]

… people still wanted ice cream. They would come in droves. 'Everyone,' Roy proclaimed, 'loves ice cream.' And, if Barton Sands was anything to go by, this will prove still to be the case. But 'things were different. My darling E.S. was different!' (Thompson)

Ezra-Sylvester took to living in the garden shed. The roses, he said, reminded him of home. It was an odd thing to say really because –

[text missing]

Sylvie gave birth to twin boys and the couple named them Sylvester-Sylvester and Ezra-Ezra, in memory of their father's lost twin and in deference to their Mediterranean heritage. The boys grew up to be red-faced, rubbery, but robust, individuals, excelling at almost nothing at school but petty theft and playground extortion.

Little else is documented about the early lives of the Maas twins, Sylvester-Sylvester and Ezra-Ezra). Though it is said by those that remember them that S.S was always kind to animals and showed a particular interest in horse husbandry (a passion that would lead him, eventually, to find stable work in a hospital for sick and decrepit steeplechasers).

The young Ezra-Ezra, as I say, was not a particularly promising student. He would be expelled by the time he was 13 for pouring paint over several teachers. However, one curious detail seems to have been saved: E.E. was an exceptional runner. Who knows where these blessings come from? Although he was, from an early age, quite a chubby child, he was, amazingly fleet of foot & became Penn Beacon County Junior School Champion short distance runner (Gold) 1957–58.

There is an intriguing photograph of Ezra-Ezra Maas (*copyright of The Barton Sands Chronicle, June 1958*) on a wall in the local history museum on Peter Street (It can be found in the corridor at the top of the stairs in the permanent exhibition called Barton Sands). Allow me to describe the image here. The photographer, one James Flasher, has positioned himself in the middle lane of the track, a few feet back from the finish line. The photograph captures the moment Maas, aged 8, bursts across the ticker tape. His head of distinctive ink stain hair is thrust towards the lens, obliterating his face. His arms are thrown up in triumph and his legs are caught forever in a blur. The photograph is of particular interest to those who enjoy social history. The crowd of onlookers that border the photograph in an almost perfect bottleneck are all turned towards the winner, and so, towards the camera itself. In the expanse of faces, can be picked out, among the usual unfortunate twisted expressions, blurred features, forever-opened mouths, and frozen, wind-blown hairstyles, is a pale and thin young boy's face. He is stood next to a woman. She has hold of his left elbow. It is jerked up awkwardly towards and beyond his shoulder. She is shouting something into his ear. He ignores her. Or (and I've looked at this picture many times), he has not quite yet, in that moment, heard her. The words are on the air. He stares directly into the camera from some feet behind the finish line and, after the winner's hair and arms and palms and the flailing trail of ticker tape, the viewer's eye is drawn directly into his. It is, and I hope this doesn't sound too, oh, I don't know, artsy, but it is as if both he is peering directly into the future. And, by the same token, you are connected to the past. There is a communication. He is Bryan Goss (later of 1980s 'art-rock' band, Dead Fox)

[*image*]

Bryan Goss of Dead Fox (1984)

How could such a rotund and ice cream fed fellow become a school champion 'short distance' (and, by this, it is meant, 100 and 200 yard distance) runner, let alone a Junior School Gold Champion? It seems incredulous, doesn't it! However, the secret to the young Ezra-Ezra's surprising success was in his style of running. It was, in nature, closer to a skip than a run. He would lead with only the left leg, all the thrust coming from the right. Young kids can be seen doing this even these days. It is the classic approximation of '*horsing around*'. Credit, I suppose, must also be given to his PE teacher at the time - Mr. D. Biscuits of Barton Sand's Junior Grammar (d. 1969), who, rather than discourage such an unorthodox style, recognised something of the genius behind it.

[*text missing*]

AUGUST 7, 1976

The church of Saint Giles is nestled one mile south of the village of Weston, Penn Beacon. There has been a church dedicated to Giles on this site since 1135AD. A simple and neglected gravestone can be found in the quiet west garden at the rear. The Penn Beacon quarried headstone reads, simply –

Ezra-Sylvester Maas.
Son. Brother. Husband. Father. Lover of Ice Cream.
September 20th 1910 – August 1976
Survived by sons Sylvester-Sylvester and Ezra-Ezra

BIBLIOGRAPHY / REFERENCES

Cornett, Desmond. *I Scream! You Scream! We All Scream For Ice Cream!* Chapterhouse Publication, 1985.

Felicini, Dr. F.D. *Gorizia! – Gas! Gas!* Roma University Press, 1957.

Gelato! The Collected Diaries of Sylvester-Ezra 1928–53, vol. 1. Templar Publications, 1977.

The Heart of Things (redux)

P M Buchan

What do the greatest writers who ever lived have in common? Samuel Taylor Coleridge. Jack Kerouac. Edgar Allen Poe. Robert Louis Stevenson. Hunter S Thompson. Can I stop there? Have you figured it out yet?

Even Stephen King battled addiction through the end of the 1970s and most of the 80s. Anyone would have to be pretty strung out to think that a rabid St Bernard is a strong enough hook to carry a 309-page novel. On his best day Stephen King could never be a truly great novelist, but just imagine how much worse his oeuvre might have been if he'd never discovered cocaine.

Great writers. Alcoholics and junkies, the lot of them, but one name towers above the rest. Daniel Ezra. Daniel fucking Ezra.

That literary giant was my hero growing up. I was too young to really understand the uproar caused by the obscenity trial following the publication of his first novel, ███████████, but not so young that I wasn't incensed by the puritanical response to a novel that was an honest appraisal of the divide between the working classes of the north east of England and the politicians, who ruled the country from far-flung stately manors and knew nothing about the reality of our lives.

Our teachers compared the release of ███████████ to Simon & Schuster dropping Bret Easton Ellis' *American Psycho* three months before it was due to be released, blaming its 'sadistic contents'. There was an author who knew how to do more than just dabble with drugs. He reported writing *Less Than Zero* on an eight-week crystal-meth binge, though conveniently spoke less at the time about the subsequent three years that it took him to make that first draft publishable. Still, Bret Easton Ellis would probably never have been published if he'd never been introduced to hard drugs, making the world a poorer place.

On reflection, we were pretty lucky to have English teachers at secondary school who were open-minded enough to even broach subjects like ███████████ with us, but then Ezra was born and bred in Newcastle, like us. He was one of our own. That first novel of his was just an appetiser for what was to come next. Critics called him the most revolutionary writer born in England since the days of Wordsworth and Coleridge, or at least, that was what they printed on his covers.

'A voyeur into humanity's dark underbelly, with appetites so blasphemous that they had no precedent.' That's what *Times Literary Supplement* said about Ezra.

So, when we spoke about the prospect of filling in our UCAS applications in Sixth Form, planning which universities to attend, a substitute teacher told us that Ezra had been given an Honorary Fellowship at Newcastle University. What's more, she said that he'd also agreed to act in an advisory role for a creative writing summer school that they were running, to encourage more of us from the local area to apply to study there.

All I'd ever wanted was to be a great writer. The greatest. I'd dreamt of that for as long as I could remember, since the first time I visited a library. Which, incidentally, is where I spent most of my childhood, avoiding the bullies in my class and escaping to other worlds while my Mam worked late, making sure we could afford somewhere to live.

It wasn't what I'd describe as a happy childhood but reading and writing got me through the worst of it. Although I earnestly wanted to be the best writer and would have done anything to improve, being a diligent student hadn't got me very far by that point. However proud my mother was of my academic success, however pleased the teachers were to have someone who took their lessons seriously, I was at best invisible to my peers. At worst? Let's just say I didn't get invited to a lot of parties.

But none of that mattered when I heard about the opportunity to sign up for a summer school that meant I'd get a guaranteed place the following year on one of the most prestigious undergraduate English Literature courses in the country and a chance to study under the Ezra, the author whose seven published novels had been shortlisted for the Booker Prize, a historic six times and winning once alongside a host of other prestigious awards.

Another reason people had picked on me at school was the seizures. It's not that I had them often, only a couple of times in secondary school, but it's like they came on at times that were designed to maximise my humiliation. This one time, getting up on stage to accept an award for an essay about the Romantics, which already marked me out as someone to shun, I took a dive so violent that the Deputy Head was dragged down underneath me.

The best writers all have crosses to bear. Edgar Allen Poe for example, people call him the originator of the detective novel. On a good day they give him credit for inventing science fiction too. It's pretty well documented that he suffered from unexpected crashes into unconsciousness, followed by agitation and confusion, which sounds a lot like seizures. And that was even before the drink and drugs started.

The first couple of times it happened, I didn't know what signs to watch out for, so when that smell like wet concrete drying after a summer rain filled my nostrils, it meant nothing. But by the week that the summer school was due to start, I recognised that smell and when I told the doctor, she sent me straight to the Royal Victoria Infirmary. They ran all kinds of different tests. The result was that I had epilepsy.

It was good to put a name on it, but there was so much time spent in hospital that by the time I arrived at the summer school, I'd missed the first week. My new classmates, they raved about Ezra's radical methods, how inspirational his lectures had been, more like sermons really. But then the remainder of the summer school was taught by one of his assistants, a weathered old walrus with a flushed face, perpetual armpit stains and the bulbous nose of an alcoholic whose best years were behind him.

Stockholm. That's what he called himself. Not Dr Stockholm, not even Mr Stockholm, just Stockholm.

We did our best to learn from the buffoon. After all, all the students who were there that summer were the writers with the most potential from the most deprived schools in the region. Every one of us had been nominated by a teacher and hand-picked as having the aptitude to succeed. But it didn't matter. Every word that we wrote was dismissed with hardly a glance by this blustering idiot. Dismissed by some third-rate sidekick who was destined to spend the remainder of his career as Ezra's dogsbody.

Worse, it's not like he was ambivalent about our work. He hated it. The criticism that Stockholm launched during our final session was so severe, so disgusted, that I began to smell that rain-on-asphalt precursor to another fit. Thunder clouds gathered in the room, making the air so dense and charged that it stunk of static. Somehow, I hung on long enough to get to the end without a seizure. Exhausted and wanting to give up on writing, give up on everything, when it was over, I tried to slink out of the classroom without being noticed.

Stockholm had just answered a black telephone on his desk, entering a heated debate with whoever was on the other end, so it should have been a simple thing to escape further criticism, but as I was passing, he thrust the phone at me with a grunt and an expression of resentment.

'...reek...sss...cadence...' The line crackled and rasped, wind rushing through a field of dry grass. 'S... m...ch... potential...sq...ndered...'

Being in a deep-sea submersible and trying to communicate with the outside world, this is how it would sound. Distant. Empty. Recognising only every third word. I was ready to hang the phone up in disappointment, but then shivered with realisation instead. Who was Stockholm here deputising for? The great Marcus Ezra. I was talking to Marcus Ezra.

More than that. I wasn't just speaking to my idol, the most popular writer that ever lived. He thought that I had potential. The crackling distortion on the line was overwhelming, but I crushed the handle of the telephone receiver with as tight a grip as I could muster and focussed on his every syllable.

'All potential but what… if you have nothing to say? How can you… never lived? …amount to naught… give… base impulses… Live boy. First, you have to live.'

Click. The voice cut off and that was the end of the phone call, after which Stockholm shooed me from the classroom, answering none of my questions and shaking his head in disgust, seemingly his default emotion.

But it was clear what Ezra had been trying to say. Technical skills were meaningless without experience to inform them. I'd been born with a gift, but any potential that I had would be squandered if I continued along the path of caution that had got me to this point. The line had broken up before I could ask him to repeat and confirm that I understood, but what else could he have meant?

By repressing my inner demons, I was denying myself a voice. How could I write about a world that I had never lived in? What could any reader learn from someone so innocent, so naive?

That night, instead of returning home to study, I tagged along with a group of the other students from the summer school to a bar downstairs from Newcastle Art Centre, called the Black Swan. Situated not far from Central Station, in the heart of Newcastle, I'd heard people talk at school about this bar that acted as a hub for local musicians and had a lax approach to checking ID, but until that day I'd never dreamt of visiting.

It wasn't long before my 17th birthday, but I was such a timid youth that the thrill as the bouncer appraised me and waved me inside was as electrifying as if I'd achieved such a feat at the age of 12. There was something about breaking the rules that I found life-affirming in ways that I couldn't have predicted. Something changed.

The rumble of bass guitars and thud of drums from live music sent tremors through my heart, welcoming me as I entered the subterranean world that was to become my home.

That night was the first time that I drank alcohol, the first time that I snorted an amphetamine and by the time I woke the next day, I had lost my virginity. The night was my epiphany.

Hubert Selby Jr, a man who was no stranger to addiction, once said he knew that two things would happen before he died; that he would regret his entire life, and that he would want to live it all over again. Well, before that night in the Black Swan I already regretted every decision that I'd ever made. And up to that point there wasn't a single moment that I would want to live over again. So, when I woke up the next day, caked in vomit and surrounded by people whose names I couldn't remember, I made a vow to indulge my desires and live a life that I really would want to live all over again.

In the weeks that followed, the summer holiday before my final year of Sixth Form, it became apparent that despite my slight frame, I had an innate capacity to tolerate alcohol, a gift that would only become more refined with practice and experience. Then, when school started again in September, there was also the discovery that I'd be able to produce work to deadline, good work, no matter how much punishment I inflicted on my body.

Rather than suffering as a result of my night-time dalliances, if anything my writing improved. Which was all the confirmation that I needed to know that Ezra had set me upon the right path.

In that final year of school my position among my peers changed. They recognised my newfound rebellion and reacted accordingly, making space to accommodate me in groups that would previously have spurned me.

My newfound social circle revolved around the son of one of the 20th century's most notorious rock stars. We called the son Sasquatch, partly because of his giant stature and wild hair, but also because of his monosyllabic tendencies and disdain for showering.

Since the death of Sasquatch's father, money had been no issue for him. There was no way of knowing how long this good fortune would last, but he took us drinking at first every weekend and before long most nights, footing the bill in the most wild and lawless nightclubs that Newcastle had to offer and as a result seemingly befriending every miscreant and drunk in the city.

Sasquatch and this new circle of friends were older, wilier, and tougher than me by far, which wasn't difficult, given my sheltered childhood. Most had dropped out of school years ago and as far as I could tell had no responsibilities or obligations to restrain them. They set an example for me to follow, but also their constant presence offered a safety net over which to experiment without fear of consequence or reprisal.

Those first pints of cheap cider with them became Snakebite, became premium-strength lager, became spirits. My first puff on a joint was soon followed by a first cigarette, then another and another. Before long magic mushrooms followed marijuana, with speed, cocaine, and ecstasy not far away.

Ecstasy, particularly, was a game-changer. I'd been a meek, self-conscious teenager, not one to speak to strangers and definitely not one to make the first move in talking to girls. Alcohol unlocked an inner confidence and charisma that had hitherto been hidden, but then ecstasy supercharged me, gave me confidence squared.

The first night that I took a pill, in Cuba Cuba of all places, probably the most squalid nightclub in the city, I pulled Sasquatch's sister to one side and gestured at all the woman on the dancefloor. All were older than me, most were taller than me, and a great many were there with boyfriends who could easily have snapped me in two. But I pulled Sasquatch's sister to one side, and I told her that I was a wolf, and they were all pieces of chicken.

Confidence was no problem from then. Female companions no longer an idle dream. Hip-hop nights at Foundation, Goth all-nighters at Rock Shots, cocktail parties at Revolution. It wasn't long until everywhere we went, I'd leave angry men baying for my blood while their girlfriends followed in my wake, safe in the knowledge that Sasquatch and the gang would protect me when things invariably went wrong. I was the youngest of the group and I flattered myself as being the most charismatic. It was only natural that they'd look out for me.

As a lonely, friendless teen I had told myself that if only I ever had the chance to make a girl happy and share my life with her then I would take it, not squander her trust like so many other boys. That feeling held for the first girl I slept with, possibly even for the second, but with newfound confidence, these passion-filled rendezvous became fleeting things. Open hearts ensnared either by the lies that ecstasy inspired me to tell or dazzled by my generosity as I helped Sasquatch to squander his inheritance. Either way, their flesh was so soft and yielding that no amount of insincerity used to secure it seemed to matter. All that mattered were my newfound appetites.

By the start of the summer that I was due to pass my A-Levels, before starting university, I'd signed with an agent who had been reluctantly recommended to me by Stockholm. The agent was a nervous little man who was all moustache, dandruff, and unrivalled literary connections. By midsummer my first collection of short stories was released, inspired by the debauchery of a hundred nights drinking every glass put in front of me and fucking everyone who would have me.

Granta sent advanced reader copies of the collection to critics around the UK and the response was mind-blowing. People began calling me Ezra's protégé, the 'Next Big Thing', before the book had even been released. The response was such that we were able to hold the launch party at The Cluny, under Newcastle's Byker Bridge, forcing London's publishing elite to travel up to the 'godforsaken north' because I refused to accommodate them by letting the capital steal our glory.

The launch was a phenomenal success, or so I was told. It was also the first night that I experienced an alcohol-induced blackout, losing several hours of what should have been the most rewarding experience of my life.

After almost a solid year of abusing Sasquatch's inheritance, due to my well-publicised deal with Granta it was time for me to repay the favour. As was traditional in our circles, it wasn't just Sasquatch and our friends who turned up at The Cluny for the launch night, it was every thirsty drunk in the city, all determined to drink the bar dry on my tab and strut around like amphetamine-fuelled peacocks in front of the London elite who we were sure thought themselves our superiors in every way.

At first their antics seemed funny. A spilled drink here, a piss on the dancefloor there. Soon it was shitting in handbags and tying people's shoelaces together, dropping urinal bleach-cakes in pint glasses and guffawing as people left to have their stomachs pumped. But these idiots had nothing to celebrate, it was my hard work and achievements that were paying for the night. I tolerated as much of their disrespect as I could stomach, but when Sasquatch set fire to the hair of the *Guardian*'s lead literary critic, there was such outcry that I had no choice but to have my friends ejected from the premises.

You wouldn't think that things could degenerate as quickly as they did in the space of a single night, but I underestimated what a powerful safety net those friends had provided. Cocktails and cocaine, absolute free fall. One minute we were toasting the health of a beautiful barmaid, the next I woke standing in a dark corner, looking down at the shards of a broken bottle while my agent clutched his face, blood pulsing between his fingers and spilling out over our feet.

'What... what happened?' I asked.

'You glassed me!'

However out of control I'd been before that incident, at least it was always possible to take credit for my own actions, by merit of remembering them. But looking at the agent, eyebrows sticky with blood, blinking at me in the half-light, there was nothing remotely familiar about the scene. No memory was forthcoming.

His claim seemed plausible, however. I'd seen the agent berate other clients with staggering viciousness when he thought that they'd stepped out of line. I wasn't so successful yet that it was beyond the realms of possibility that he had spoken to me thus, berating me for jeopardising the launch with my bad behaviour.

Whatever the truth, seeing him like that was a disturbing development. I'd been a pacifist all my life until that point, or at least, my predisposition and physical prowess had never leant themselves to violence. But seeing the fruits of my labour, smelling the iron tang of his blood, filled me with shame.

Did I really have the kind of brain that could allow me to hurt someone and then rewrite my memories to mask my actions?

Someone alerted the bouncers, who approached the agent to help him, as I crept away, one tentative step at a time at first, before turning heel and running through the night streets of Byker. Blundering through the darkness, it felt like there was no avenue for hope, nobody to ask for help. Not after so decisively jettisoning Sasquatch.

But then I remembered that it was Stockholm who had recommended me to the agent in the first place, so I stopped at the first phone box I could find and fished his business card out of my wallet. The phone rang and rang, each tone signalling desolation, but then miraculously Stockholm answered.

'Put him on,' I demanded.

'How dare you presume to speak to me that way? Boy, when your star has long faded and the novelty of your preposterous existence has been forgotten, I'll still be here. In fact...'

Someone spoke to Stockholm in the background. Too far away for me to recognise, but I could hope.

'Hang up,' he said. 'Wait there and don't move.'

I did as I was told, wondering whether I had gone too far. Not even a year had passed since the summer school, which now divided my life into the periods before and after. The two periods were so far apart as to be almost irreconcilable. But I was trying.

The path to greatness was never going to be an easy one. The great Jack Kerouac struggled with addiction right up to his death, veering from alcohol to Benzedrine and everything in between. He once said that 'the best teacher is experience,' which is a sentiment that I chose to subscribe to, for better or worse.

You could make an argument that the success of 'On the Road' ruined him, but then on the other hand you could also say that it has been translated into 32 languages, over 4-million copies have been sold to date and that booksellers still consistently sell over 100,000 English-language copies every year, which is proof that Kerouac's sacrifice was worth it.

Finally, the telephone in the booth rang.

'I've done a terrible thing,' I said.

'Go on,' said my hero.

I explained everything that had happened since he advised me to truly live. The good and the bad. As a man clearly drawn to the darker spectrum of human behaviour, I hoped that Ezra would be able to offer some practical advice about how to limit my future transgressions.

What a fucking fool I was.

'Good,' he said, his voice ringing out with glee.

Yet again, the voice sounded a great distance away. I strained to hear his wisdom over the buzzing of flies and the roar of traffic passing over Byker Bridge.

'I've been following your work,' the voice said. 'Stockholm... appraised. Of course, he... But you're approaching the heart of things now, faster than I could have hoped. The thing to remember is... And don't forget Blake's words. The fool who persists in his folly will become wise.'

Then he began to laugh, the sound echoing around my head in circles as I cradled the phone in my hand and fell to my knees. After that, everything went black.

The launch party at The Cluny marked a turning point for me. Granta discredited the claims of my agent, who thought that he could coerce me into paying for plastic surgery to fix what was never much more than a scratch in the first place. Sales of my collection rocketed, so it was no problem finding another agent.

It would have been such a simple thing to find Sasquatch and our other friends, to apologise for kicking them out of the party to save face. But why should I apologise to those jackasses? Their futures were laid out for the world to see, smoking weed and playing Grand Theft Auto in between visits to the Job Centre. They'd never amount to anything, but my name was written in the stars.

People like them, with no vision or ambition, were the reason that Newcastle was and always will be a shithole. So yes, I could have apologised to them and gone back to my old life, but I was ready for the next chapter, so instead I followed my editor's advice and moved to London. I traded Westgate Road for Islington, moving closer to the source.

In parallel with my own success, Marcus Ezra had begun to transcend from merely a bestselling writer to become one of the best-paid artists of all time. I was following the trail that he blazed, hot on his heels. As my readership grew, his success grew in tandem.

London started innocently enough. After a period of such excess, starting anew in another city felt like an opportunity to reinvent myself, away from familiar faces and the temptation that they represented. The short stories had found an audience, so now it was time to focus on my first novel, which I wanted to be a scathing attack on the hypocrisy that everyone in society seemed intent on wallowing in.

When I sat down to write, mercifully the prose came without effort. But then whenever I put down my pen, so did the hedonism, spurred on by a new scene of literary hangers-on who were desperate to be seen with me and associated with this new wave of literary hellraisers.

Without the bonds of friendship that I had depended on in Newcastle, I became lost, adrift in a hell of my own manufacture. But wasn't that what I had been aiming for in the first place? I mean, between 1933 and 1937 F Scott Fitzgerald was hospitalised for alcoholism eight times, before his death at the ripe old age of 44. But did you ever read *The Great Gatsby*? Whatever Fitzgerald had to sacrifice to write that book, it was worth it.

So, the blackouts, which started in The Cluny, became more than sporadic occurrences. If you've never been blackout drunk before, let me explain how it works. The first time it happens, you might wake in bed and not remember anything after arriving at the nightclub the night before. It's a yawning black hole, you have no way of reaching into that absence to ascertain what happened to you, unless some bumbling halfwit recounts your antics to you and the shame washes down from head to toe, as surely as if they'd cracked an egg over you.

That's how the blackouts start, but once you're into the creep, the period you can't remember begins to expand. In the beginning, I'd lose the journey home from a nightclub, a few minutes in a black cab or a late-night hour in a karaoke booth. But soon I'd lose whole nights, whole days, my body's way of hiding truths that my mind wasn't ready to accept.

Whatever I put up my nose and however much I drank, I always managed to write, because there was so much to write about. The release of my first novel met almost universal acclaim, or that was what my editor and agent told me. In the wake of the release, touring the interview circuit for newspapers, radio, and television, it seemed as if I had a handle on my appetites.

There was a beautiful period dallying with a mesmerising, green-eyed model who used the name Juliette Strange. She was the illegitimate daughter of two of the most celebrated film stars of the 1990s, mercifully disowned by her father, who was later revealed to be an abusive womaniser with an army of handlers whose jobs were to cushion him from the consequences of his actions.

Juliette caught my eye on the catwalk at Paris Fashion Week and we became fast friends, trading on my notoriety to experience the most wild and extravagant decadence that some of the biggest cities in the world had to offer. She was a wild bird finally uncaged, a fever dream. Our love for each other burned with such intensity and ferocity that nobody in our orbit escaped unscathed.

It was the British tabloids that killed her in the end, hounding her from one den of iniquity to the next, until our usual dealer was exposed to too much scrutiny and arrested. We found another connection easily enough, but the junk that he sold us was poison. I went out one night without her, ironically enough to the opening of the Nu-Viper Lounge and returned to our hotel room to find her face down in a pool of blood and vomit, with a needle hanging out of her arm.

If I had been there to throw ice water on her face, or even phone an ambulance, things might have been different, but instead she died alone, and I lived. Ostensibly.

Somehow this very public shame did nothing to tarnish my reputation. If anything, book sales increased after Juliette's death. My popularity grew in proportion to my transgressions. More invitations to speak on TV, more interviews, more kudos. But without Juliette, I sought companionship in all the wrong places, taking on a long line of sidekicks who inevitably hoped to further their careers by association with me. They wanted me to do for them what Ezra had done for me.

We'd start as drinking buddies in Camden, the best of friends in a community populated by aspiring artists and failures who couldn't bring themselves to stop chasing long-dead dreams. Pints of Estrella, Jägerbombs, endless lines of coke. But these impressionable fools were too eager to make names for themselves, downing too many drinks, picking fights to impress me, losing control, and having nothing to show for it at the end.

These sidekicks and protégés had short shelf-lives and inevitably wound up jailed or worse, succumbing to collapsed septums, blood poisoning, infective endocarditis, turning up on my doorstep in the middle of the night begging for one more drink, one more hit, one more chance.

However far they fell, I went faster and further. It got to the point where it wasn't a night out if I hadn't pissed myself or woke choking on vomit. It didn't matter how far I travelled, the cities blurred into one, shuffling from one crack den to the next, completely dependent on heroine. The honeymoon period of shooting up to get high became a distant dream, I became a lumbering beast, desperate always for the next fix just to get well.

Shuffling through the motions on interviews, I took to wearing long sleeves to hide the tracks on my arm, scarves to hide the bruises around my neck. Sunglasses at night, hiding from the daylight, I was a pallid wreck, mottled with infected injection-sites, but I knew better than to shoot up between my fingers like some. My hands, I saved, so that it didn't matter if the paparazzi caught me asleep behind the wheel or face down in some Michelin Star Restaurant, so long as I could still write there was always someone to make excuses for my actions. I could do no wrong.

For every blank page that I filled, another of my sins would be forgiven. For every acerbic word, another budding young writer lit up with admiration. I satisfied every dark urge imaginable and wrote about it all, until I no longer recognised the face looking back at me in the mirror. No longer knew my own name.

Every goal I set, I accomplished. Everything I'd ever dreamt of was within my reach. But there was still one obstacle left for me to overcome. Everywhere I went, my mentor and hero Ezra was one step ahead of me. There were no paths left for me to travel that he hadn't mastered long before I arrived.

Every significant moment of my life, he had been there in the shadows, whispering and spurring me on to greatness. But what was the point if I'd always be in his shadow?

At the height of my fame, our two names were invariable mentioned in the same breath, blistering prophets of the end times, but his was always held in the highest esteem. He the master and I the pupil.

Ezra. The old fool once felt so vital to my art, such an inspiration, but his success became a tumour nestled in my own happiness. He was a blight on my continued relevance. The figurehead of an obsolete generation. If my voice was ever going to be recognised as the final truth, then he would have to agree to retire and cease spreading what by now were nothing more than tired, redundant platitudes.

I resolved to confront him. He'd had his day, now it was time to practice what he had preached in his youth and stand aside for the next generation. Surely, he could not argue with such logic, with the words that he himself had written?

Ezra agreed to meet me in the Three Coffins, one of the last pubs in the country that could demonstrably be relied upon for discretion when I visited. I'd long since tired of journalists with no scruples profiting by publishing photographs of me doing research for my art.

Hunter S Thompson, that brilliant, deranged gonzo journalist, once said 'I hate to advocate drugs, alcohol, violence, or insanity to anyone, but they've always worked for me.' On the night that Ezra met me face-to-face for the first time, those words echoed in my ears.

I'd been drinking heavily that day, as I did every day, and had already strayed far from inhibitions by the time he slid into the booth and sat opposite me. Our first drink together was strained, the second more cordial, the third, fourth and fifth were riotous celebrations of our joint accomplishments. As I grew in courage over the course of the night, I steeled myself to suggest that he abdicate his throne voluntarily before I was forced to take matters into my own hands.

The lights in the bar flickered and thunder boomed in the distance, right before the rain began to fall. I could smell the raindrops as they hit the street, filling the cracks between the warm paving slabs, evaporating almost as soon as they appeared. It filled my nostrils, electricity in the air. A seizure was coming on, an inescapable juggernaut looming on the horizon and running towards me full force, all hurried legs and claws and clacking mandibles.

I must have blacked out, falling headfirst into the dark mire of subconscious, haunted by strobing images that were impossibly, achingly insistent. In dreams, I harangued my hero to come back to my apartment, where I offered friendship, pouring him a drink, and in return he laughed at the mockery of a man I had become and berated me for misinterpreting his advice.

Ezra said that I had sacrificed my talents for baubles, for adulation that poisoned my mind and rendered my writing impotent and derivative. He bared his crooked teeth, threw back his head and laughed, spraying spittle all over the cocktail bar. He had the nerve to say that he had seen such potential in my work, my innocence, but that now there was nothing left that could be salvaged.

He grabbed my wrist, leering at me, fingers grinding my bones together. Lost in the logic of dreams I fought to free myself from his influence, to break the surface for air, until I experienced what felt like my first lucid thought in months. I had been deceived. It wasn't Ezra who had come to meet me, it was Stockholm, with his bulbous nose and broken capillaries, his halitosis, and reeking armpits.

How many times had I been deceived this same way, making do with the dancing puppet when what I needed was the one pulling the strings?

It was too much, trying to focus through this shimmering mirage. Ezra and Stockholm's faces merged into one, their laughter dragging me through the streets of public humiliation, flagellating me on the road to Golgotha. They laughed and laughed and laughed, disgusting braying donkeys, until the flashing of Ezra's nicotine-stained teeth and the bark of his ugly voice threatened to swallow me whole.

I moved as if underwater, lashing out, shrieking at the top of my lungs and sobbing, wailing, anything to drown out that insidious laughter, but nothing that I did could dampen his merriment. Not fingernails to gouge tracks across his badly shaven cheeks, not ribs cracking beneath the stamp of my feet, not jaws and teeth to bite and rend mouthfuls of bitter, rancid flesh. Nothing could entreat him to silence, not the sizzling stink of burnt skin on the gas hob, not the hot spiral of viscera spilling from an abdominal cavity that must have been bigger on the inside than the outside.

The dreams were chaos, completely implausible, screams and laughter indistinguishable from one another. When I woke from this sepulchral vision, Ezra's last breath of final choking words rung in my hears, over and over.

'Ever have I effortlessly pulled your strings.'

But surely it was a dream, a nightmare, the delirium tremens of an overworked writer, fighting to hit his next deadline? Because the apartment was spotless when I woke, gleaming with the chemical burn of bleach. The sinks shone; the floors polished to perfection. Only a single, nicotine-stained molar on the bathroom floor suggested that anything untoward could have taken place.

I am now something more, and something less, than I was born. Though I walk upright like a man, though I remember the correct way to reply when you call my name, there is a hole in my heart that can never be filled, a hunger so deep and all-consuming that I fear even Hell itself will hold no surprises for me.

The staff employed by my most recent publisher continue to shield me from the consequences of my actions, but I am a prisoner now in my own home. By accident or design, I can never leave, forced to continue my work but never again to feel sunlight on my cheek or wind in my hair.

My minders no longer humour my whims as they once did, tasked only with ensuring that I continue to write, but no more than that. I try to engage them in conversation, but they evade any attempts to question them. I ask, sometimes directly and sometimes obliquely, about my mentor, Ezra. Sometimes I even ask about that flatulent idiot who assisted him, Stockholm. The faces of my minders and assistants are always guarded, but I swear that neither the mention of Ezra nor Stockholm's names elicit any glint of recognition in their eyes.

Cut off from the outside world, I don't know whether Ezra survived our encounter on that last night together or not. It is becoming increasingly difficult to find the inspiration to write. There was a time when I would pore over the works of my mentor and find there the spark that I needed to light my imagination, but all of his books have been taken from me and there seems to be no one left who remembers the great man or his work.

Every day the minders employed by my publisher become more heavy-handed, deflecting my questions with pills and injections, but no matter how dull my reflexes become, I can't stop asking myself the question. Who was Ezra?

There was a time, long ago, when people valued my words. When I thought that I was free. But now, I am so utterly disconnected from the world that any thought of the past feels increasingly like fiction.

Ezra ruined my life as surely as I ruined his. I write these words, as unlikely as they sound, because if Ezra has been written out of history, then might I not be next?

What do the greatest artists who ever lived have in common? They're all dead. Mostly, they died young. However successful or not they were in their lifetimes is nothing compared to the acclaim that we shower them with in death. They had to die for their words to live on.

Ezra is nothing now but a ghost. If I'm cunning and discrete, just maybe I can keep a record of his greatness and help him to maintain a foothold in the world. Doing so might be the only way to save myself.

The process of elimination has already begun. Every night, the nurses prise this notepad from my fingers and the next day when they return it to me the pages are blank.

They pretend that the pages were always empty, but I know the truth.

Every night, I write this story anew.

My thoughts are clouded now, harder, and harder to retain. There are so many distractions. So many ways and reasons to forget.

Through thick fog I write these words, watching even now as they fade without a trace.

To those who follow me I say, you must attempt to fall faster and further than I ever managed.

Perhaps, before your death, you will do what I could not. Perhaps you will get to the heart of things.

E.M.

Meaghan Ralph

Rushing rushing rushing reds everywhere streaks of yellow everywhere lights bouncing all around. I was drunk and in the chaotic movements found myself on the 1-train platform from Penn station going uptown to the Bronx. The 1 is like a local bus, every, 30, feet, you, stop. I was with a group of people and the thought of the 45-minute ride held no appeal. As we all got onto the train I saw a man of an indefinable quality. I could never pick him out of a crowd but the briefcase he was carrying was eye-catching. There was a silver plaque with the inscription 'E.M.' I watched him get off the train as I was jostled on. In that moment I bolted. People shouted after me but the doors closed and I was on the other side.

I scanned the emptying platform for my mystery stranger still wobbling from all the whiskey sours. I thought I saw him and decided to follow him, as I ascended the stairs out of the station he was gone. I was alone, drunk, and my anticipated adventure had disappeared. There was nothing left for it but to walk home which was only a few blocks and a couple avenues I told myself to avoid spending cash on a taxi. I would walk it. And at the end I would meet my bed, and would likely smoke some cigarettes and hope the world would stop spinning. Above ground the lights were back to rushing the same reds and yellows bouncing all over the place. As I began walking home I felt a hand grab my arm, I turned and was met with a mild looking man who was shorter then myself. He gave me a half smile, which I returned unsure of what was happening. The next thing I knew I was being pushed to my knees, this man who was just standing in front of a bar was forcing himself on me. I didn't know what to do and tried to stand up but was pushed down again. In this city of a million people, I was not seen. I was not heard. I refused to be forced so I turned it into my decision. My prerogative. I got up and stumbled away into the darkness of the avenue, off the street.

The lights were so infrequent and just that streetlight yellow. I had come to 9th avenue and just need to walk down 9 streets. I put my hand in my purse to look for a cigarette and pulled out a piece of paper. The mild monster had at some point given me his phone number. I just wanted to sleep and forget. When I got home, I decided to climb up to the roof. My apartment was right over the highline, so I could see the people walking the park or look up and see the sky. Above & below. While I puffed on my third cigarette in a row, I looked down scanning the park. Something glinted and from the distance I could see I had found my briefcase man. He was sitting on park bench, whether he was watching the world or lost in his own I could not tell. But I could swear at one point he looked up and saw me.

The Master[81]

translated by Ian Roden

The KGB had kept their eye on the Maas Foundation from its inception, suspicious of its opaque objectives, secrecy, and influence, which appeared far greater than might ordinarily be expected from an artistic foundation, albeit a fabulously wealthy one. So it was, deep into a rainy night in 1975, that a car with diplomatic plates pulled up on a side street near to the Orsteds Park in Copenhagen, and Junior Cultural Attaché from the Soviet Embassy, Sergei Antonov, slipped out, immediately disappearing among the sparse groups of late night revellers.

After half an hour of circuitous wandering to ensure he hadn't picked up a tail from PET – the Danish Intelligence Service – Sergei finally reached his target: a five storey office block of glass and steel, filling the space left in a row of handsome 18th century townhouses by a World War 2 bomb dropped some 30 years before.

---

[81]. 'The Master' by Janos Paulson (1957–93) originally published in December 1992 edition of *Nquiry* magazine. Reproduced by kind permission of the estate of the author.

The young KGB officer lit a cigarette and held it in an underhand pinch so the glow wouldn't illuminate the spare, dark features of his face.

No lights showed in the office windows. The place appeared entirely deserted.

A heavy set man in a lopsided parka with rain-sodden nylon fur trimmed hood stopped by Sergei and asked him for a light. Sergei gave him a box of British 'Pioneer' matches.

'Keep it,' Sergei said in Russian accented Danish. 'I've got another box.'

The heavy set man nodded and sloped off, leaving behind a faint whiff of stale sweat and damp, manmade fibre.

A couple of minutes later, a van pulled up by the office block and regurgitated two men from its rear doors before disappearing into the night.

Sergei walked over the road to the men; Borzoi – long faced, middle-aged and watchful – and Uri – wheezy, hunched, and florid, with rodent-like black eyes staring out from behind steamed up glasses perched on a boxer's nose.

The young officer knew both men by reputation from Moscow Centre but had never worked with the famed break-in team before.

'You Oleg's boy?' Whispered Borzoi clearly not impressed by what he saw.

'I'm attached to Comrade Gordovski's office, yes,' replied Sergei, quietly, prompting a snort from the Uri.

'I got socks older than you. How the fuck you make Captain so quickly? You sucking Oleg's dick?'

Sergei took a measured step toward Uri. 'No, but I hear it tastes of your Mum,' he replied.

Uri and Borzoi exchanged dangerous looks then burst into silent laughter, their shoulders shaking.

'You cheeky fucker,' said Uri. 'You got some balls on you, I'll give you that.'

'No hair on them,' said Borzoi. 'But you'll do.'

The three men reached the office block and looked around. The street was deserted.

Borzoi quickly reviewed the front door leading through to a marble walled lobby.

'Prelims say there are no cameras, an alarm system from a DIY store and some old codger of a guard who spends most of the night asleep in the basement. The weakest security of all the Maas Foundation offices.'

'Locks are fucking works of art though,' said Uri. 'Swiss made, very expensive. Unpickable and unbreakable, unless you have a fucking tank handy. The first choice for every rich, capitalist bastard with a secret to hide.'

Sergei's shoulders slumped. This was not going to be an easy operation.

'Good job the boss of the company is such an appalling pervert,' said Borzoi. 'The pictures we have of that filthy old bugger. They'd make even Uri's mother blush.'

'I take it we've got his dick in a vice?' Said Sergei.

Uri nodded and with a theatrical flourish produced an elaborate looking key made of dull, black metal. 'The Master,' he said. 'This beauty can unlock every boutique bank, lakeside palace and exclusive law firm in Europe.'

Sergei smiled. 'Are you old lads usually this... Dramatic?' He asked as Uri applied The Master to the lobby door lock, eliciting an expensive sounding clunk from within the mechanism.

'It's not often we have an audience,' said Borzoi as the men slipped into the heavily shadowed lobby.

'Especially not one of you ballet boys,' said Uri. 'Aren't you supposed to be fabricating your expenses and chatting up radical, rich-girl students at artsy-fartsy cultural exchange dos?'

'It's not a PR Line job,' said Sergei. 'Orders come straight from the Rezident.'

Borzoi nodded. Uri's rodent eyes regarded Sergei unblinkingly.

'Which are?'

Sergei didn't reply. He was too absorbed by what he saw in the liminal gloom of the lobby.

'Black Portoro marble,' he whispered. 'The walls, the desk, everything. That's like two thousand dollars a square metre.'

'It's fucking creepy,' said Uri. 'Makes Lenin's tomb look like a discotheque.'

'The miracle of capitalism; the cost of a hospital on the walls of a lobby no one is allowed into unless they're loaded,' said Borzoi. 'Come on. Let's burn these fuckers.'

'Which brings me back to my original question,' said Uri. 'What are the orders?'

Sergei broke out a small flashlight and began sweeping the lobby desk. 'Names, contacts, objectives. Anything that tells us what Maas wants, from whom and for what reasons.'

'Hem, why?' Said Borzoi.

'Because we know nothing about them. Not clue one. They're a complete enigma. That sort of secrecy in itself is interesting.'

'We think they're a front?' Said Uri.

Sergei nodded. 'Gotta be. CIA probably. Only the Yanks got the travellers' cheques to purchase this sort of flash. They funded artists like Jackson Pollock to turn the intelligentsia away from the revolution. This is probably more of the same; a way to reach into the European art world and recruit opinion makers their cause.'

'You hear that, Borzoi?' Said Uri. 'Sharpen your brushes, we're on the frontline of the culture wars.

Uri shot a grin at his partner, the smile morphing into something more serious as he took in Borzoi's suddenly alert and watchful expression.

'S'up pal?'

Borzoi held a finger to his lips. He then touched an ear, pointed to a corridor left of the lobby and held up one finger.

The three men dropped behind the desk and listened.

All they could hear was the faint patter of rain against the smoked glass of the office block windows.

'You need to cut down on that Danish coffee,' whispered Uri. 'No one here but us Russians.'

Sergei took a deep breath and truly listened; coldly analysing every impression of sound his sharp ears picked up. Nothing. And yet, something. Almost the sense of an object around which the white noise of the rain was passing.

He hazarded a glance around the desk toward the corridor but saw nothing but shadow and the glow of a call switch for an elevator.

Ding! The door of the elevator opened, spilling light into the corridor. No one got out. After several years the doors closed with a precise whirr and clunk.

'It was the lift, you jumpy sod,' Uri hissed at Borzoi. 'They got to keep moving automatically to stop the mechanisms from seizing.'

Borzoi looked less than convinced.

Beyond the free standing marble wall behind the lobby desk stood concrete and steel stairs leading to the upper floors.

Sergei pointed to them. 'Shall we?'

Uri shot another glance at Borzoi then nodded. 'Come on.'

Borzoi complied, but never took his eyes of the corridor until it was out of sight.

The first floor was less upmarket than the lobby, with utility grey carpet and a white walled, unlit corridor into which opened small offices and meeting rooms.

'You got another master key?' Sergei asked Borzoi, who responded with a nod.

'Good. Have a snoop about around here. 'Uri and I will take the next floor.'

Borzoi paused, then acknowledged with a brief salute of his index finger.

'Just give a squawk on the WT if you find anything,' said Uri, pulling a small two-way radio from his pocket.

'Radio silence though,' said Sergei, eliciting a look of irritation from Borzoi; which the younger officer found more reassuring than the notoriously tough agent's recent jitteriness.

The corridor to the second floor was hidden by a large double door just beyond the lift entrance.

The route to the stairs for the third floor was blocked by a metal door that would have been more suited to the bulkhead of a submarine. Uri ran his torch briefly over it, pushed his woollen hat back on his head and let out a quiet whistle.

'Now that's a fucking door,' he said. 'Electronic combination lock, anti-drill, anti-tamper, motion alarm and eight deadbolts. Torch job… If you have about five hours.'

'What the hell have they got up there?'

'Fuck knows,' whispered Uri. 'But you're right. This ain't no art institute. That's state actor engineering.'

Sergei pulled a low-light compact camera from his coat pocket and took a couple of shots of the door.

'This is just what we're looking for. Suggest we exfiltrate now, get eyes and analysts on this place.'

'Agreed, Captain,' said Uri, perhaps a little too quickly, making Sergei wonder what was making the two hardest of hard-nuts out of Central so jumpy. Though he had to admit, there was something about the tasteful, rich, sterile design of the place that was starting to nag at his guts.

Uri's radio emitted a quiet squawk of static.

'Borzoi,' said Uri looking at the radio, puzzled.

The squawk was followed by several more.

'Shit, is he in trouble?' Said Sergei.

'He better be,' said Uri, heading back down the stairs. 'Windy fucker's been a bag of nerves since we got burned in Cologne last year.'

Sergei followed. Cologne? He'd heard rumours a team got caught in a shoot out with West German cops who had mistaken them for Baader-Meinhof. Was that Borzoi and Uri?

They reached the first floor and made their way down the corridor.

'Borzoi,' hissed Uri. 'Borzoi, where the fuck are you?'

Borzoi burst out of an office door, straight in front of Sergei and Uri.

'Fuck's sake, man!' Said Uri, pulling his punch and giving Borzoi a push on the shoulder. 'What you playing at?'

'Follow me,' hissed Borzoi.

'No,' said Sergei. 'We've got what we came for.'

Borzoi shook his head. 'Follow me,' he insisted. 'It's important.'

Uri looked to Sergei, who paused, then nodded.

They followed Borzoi into an office full of shadows and expensive looking office furniture. Copenhagen twinkled dimly through the smoked, floor to ceiling windows.

'Got in with this,' said Borzoi indicating The Master, held on a chain around his neck. 'Only lock that needed it on this floor.'

'So, what's the deal? You thinking of decorating your flat like this and wanted our opinion?' Asked Borzoi.

Borzoi produced a small flashlight and played the beam on the wall, where it picked out a cluster of framed paintings and sketches.

Sergei gasped and stepped forward to more closely examine the pictures.

'Saints in heaven,' he said. 'That's a Bruegel.'

'A preparatory sketch for the Death of the Virgin,' said Borzoi.

'Circa 1564,' replied Uri. 'Looted by the Nazis from the Parisian home of a Jewish doctor in 1941. Part of a hoard of stolen paintings that went missing in Poland in 1945.'

Sergei looked hard at the two men, surprise turning to suspicion. 'I thought I was the only Ballet Boy around here? What's going on?'

The two older men looked equally non-plussed.

'It's what we were looking for in Cologne,' said Uri. 'Before the cops turned up and started a fucking recreation of the Siege of Leningrad.'

'We had to memorise the entire catalogue of of the hoard before the op,' said Borzoi. 'No one said why, we figured we were chasing old Nazis.'

Sergei examined the other pictures; an early impression of The Knight, Death and the Devil by Durer, a Cezanne still life and...

'Degas. Incredible.'

'Sold for 10,000 francs in 1898,' said Borzoi. 'Probably looking at 100,000 dollars, right there.'

'There's a massive vault door blocking the way to the third floor,' said Uri. 'Guess we know what's behind it now.'

Borzoi looked at Sergei. 'Shit. If it's the Polish hoard, that's about 100 million dollars' worth of Nazi loot.'

The intelligence men stared at each other in the gloom, their faces buried in shadow as they pieced together the evidence.

'Don't say it's a fucking bank,' said Uri.

An off-kilter smile broke on Borzoi's face. 'The CIA are using art stolen off the Jews by the Nazis as collateral to fund off-the-books ops?'

Sergei shot a look at the two men. 'That's a hell of a leap from a big door and a handful pictures,' he said. 'Get a grip, boys. Come on. Borzoi, watch the door. Uri hold a light on those pictures while I get a few shots.'

'Yeah?' Said Uri, complying. 'If it's such a big leap, then why's Central had us memorising inventory? Why the Rezident himself send a cultural attaché who actually knows something about culture to break in?'

'Only one reason,' said Borzoi. 'Our boys have got the scent.'

'So how did the CIA get their hands on the hoard?' Asked Sergei as he lined up the Degas in the viewfinder of his camera.

'When the Great Patriotic War was nearly over,' said Borzoi. 'OSS were snatching all the useful Nazis they could find and spiriting them away to America. Like von Braun. That's how they got a man on the moon and a bunch of ICBMs pointing at Mother Russia.'

'Maybe one of those pet OSS fascists was the SS Ober-gruppenführer in charge of the Polish hoard. Traded the whereabouts for a passport out of Nuremberg.'

'Think of it,' said Uri, almost giddy. 'One match to this place and we could kill the funding on the Company's most secret operations and leave their Director with a bunch of unsupported loans he'd need to explain to a Senate that already hates the CIA for spying on them. We could finish them.'

'We'll be fucking legends,' said Borzoi.

'You two need to get a hold of yourselves,' said Sergei, pocketing the camera. 'We ghost out of here, handover the evidence to the Rezident, keep our mouths shut and let the big brains in Central work out what Maas is.'

A heavy, metallic grinding noise echoed down the corridor, followed by a loud boom.

The men shut up and instinctively ducked. Uri switched off the flashlight.

'The vault door,' said Sergei.

'Someone working late?' Said Uri. The men made their way warily to the office door and peered down the gloomy corridor towards the stairway.

Borzoi put a finger to his lips. Tapped his ear.

The men listened. The sound of rain on the window. The distant susurration of the city at night. And then.

Tap. Tap. Tap. The sound of feet. Tiny feet. Tiny feet, descending the stairs.

'A woman,' whispered Uri.

The footsteps stopped at the first floor. The hint of a small, paler shadow manifested itself at the corridor's end. It remained very still.

To Sergei, the rain seemed louder now. Even the silence had its own oppressive feel; black, empty and sterile, smelling faintly of paint and bleach and new carpets.

Tap. The pale shadow took a step into the corridor.

Sergei pushed his hand into a coat pocket and found the sap he carried by way of protection. His hand closed around its handle.

Tap. Tap.

The shadow took two further steps toward the men.

Sergei thought he caught the whirr of something precise and mechanical, like clockwork. Then a sound of something so mundane and yet so out of place it forced a gasp out the three KGB men.

Birdsong. Like a lark.

'What the fuck?' Hissed Uri.

'Lock the door on it,' said Sergei.

Uri nodded. Borzoi suppressed a laugh.

The men retreated back into the office and Uri closed the door with a quiet click. Then turned the Master in the lock.

The tumblers fell into place with a clack, like a rifle bolt being pulled back.

Tap. Tap. Tap. The footsteps grew closer and more insistent. Whatever it was, it had heard them.

Sergei pulled out the sap. Uri caught sight of it, nodded. Borzoi was now openly laughing, but his eyes were bulging with fear.

Something flitted briefly past the oblong of the glass window set in the office door.

The handle of the door clunked up and down. Stopped.

There was a long, heavy silence.

And then the door burst open with a splintering crash as if it had been hit by a truck and a figure stepped into the doorway.

Sergei dropped the sap. His mouth moved but no sound came out. Uri made a little, strangled cry. Borzoi's laughter grew less controlled.

Before them, cast in the dull light from the office windows, was a ballet dancer; an automaton, dressed in a tutu gone papery with age and stained silk ballet shoes. Its face was that of a child no more than thirteen, the hair tied back, the eyes black, the lips drawn to show tiny, porcelain teeth from behind which came another burst of lark song. The automaton turned its soulless gaze toward the men. The grin grew wider. Then, with a shriek it began to move toward them in jerky movements, its dusty, brass fingers extended like talons.

TRANSCRIPT #001[82]

Fade In:

SUPER: Moscow August 21st 1991

The CLUNK and BEEP of an old school
video camera being switched on.
Indistinct RUSTLING and MUTTERING.

Darkness, then rolling lines of VIDEO
STATIC, resolving itself into a...

INT. SOVIET ERA MOSCOW APARTMENT - DAY

We see the action from the POV of a
video camera, complete with visual
noise associated with old VHS stock.

[82.] Transcript and description taken from videos recorded by Janos Paulson and Alex Tiago, Moscow August 21–22 1991. Subject: Colonel Maksim Cherkshin – KGB, Maas and Operation ROOK.

JANOS PAULSON - 30 something, dark,
dressed like a cheap PI from a 50s
movie - looks out of a grubby window.

                    JANOS
              (beckons to camera)
         Alex.

The camera moves to the window.

INT/EXT. MOSCOW STREET - DAY

We see RED ARMY SOLDIER 1 and RED ARMY
SOLDIER 2 run down an otherwise empty
Moscow street.

Distant sound of SEMI-AUTOMATIC GUNFIRE.
Then the BOOM of a tank shell.

                    ALEX (O.C.)
         Shit.

                    MAX (O.C.)
              (wheezy laugh)
         Weather getting worse, boys?

INT. SOVIET-ERA MOSCOW APARTMENT - DAY

Alex turns the camera to face.

MAKSIM 'MAX' CHERKASHIN (70). A big man
gone to skin and bones, buried in an old
cardigan covered with cigarette burns.
He wears a CANNULA in his nose.

Max sits in a cheap, high backed chair
next to a TANK OF OXYGEN in a cluttered
and untidy apartment living room/kitchen.

Max's laughter breaks into a wracking
cough.

                    JANOS
          Can I get you something, Max?

Max waves Janos away and takes a huff of
oxygen from a MASK.

                    MAX
          Get on with it. We're all short of
          time.

Janos nods, takes a seat opposite Max.

                    JANOS
                 (to camera)
          Janos Paulson interviewing Colonel
          Maksim Cherkashin about Operation
          Rook - session five.

                    (to Max)
You were the lookout for Operation
ROOK in Copenhagen the night three
KGB officers disappeared inside
the Maas Institute.

                    MAX
Yes. Yes. We've already established
that. I watched Sergei, Uri and
Borzoi go in and stood watch until
sunrise.

                    JANOS
When did you know something was
wrong?

                    MAX
Almost straight off. The radio didn't
work, no telephone nearby and we
were at least three men short.
The whole operation was a shambles.

                    JANOS
You raised the alarm, when?

                    MAX
First light, when finally someone
came to see where we'd got to.

                    JANOS
You never established what happened
to them?

                    MAX
Turns out the building was empty.
Maas had cleared out a couple
of days before. More bad intel.
Got so I fell under suspicion.
Must have told my story a hundred
times back at Central. Thought
my number was up.

                    JANOS
So, if you never entered the
building and the officers just
disappeared, where did you get
all that detail about the looted
paintings and the ballet dancer?

                    MAX
                (grim smile)
Ah. Well. Two weeks later,
Sergei just turned up at the
Embassy. Looked like he'd spent
the last year in a tree.

                    ALEX (O.C.)
I thought you said they were all
dead.

                    MAX
They are. Uri and Borzoi washed
up in the harbour. Cause of death
unknown. Sergei... Well he died in
a secure KGB psychiatric unit
about seven years back.

                    JANOS
He was mad?

                    MAX
As shit house rat. But he had moments
of lucidity, especially when we
talked. And after the psych-docs
had shot him up with God knows what.

                    JANOS
You debriefed Sergei?

                    MAX
Yeah. Took a few years. But I
finally got enough to make a
plausible story.

                    JANOS
  (not without hint of irony)
You think a hoard of stolen master-
pieces, guarded by a automaton for
the CIA sounds plausible?

                    MAX
              (laugh cough)
    They found very small traces of
    psilocybin in Sergei's clothes.

                  DAN (O.C.)
    Magic Mushrooms?

                    MAX
    It's puzzle, isn't it? Wouldn't
    be the first case of psychedelic
    incapacitation. It was the seventies.
    I'm guessing gas pumped through
    the AC. It'd explain the erratic
    behaviour and the hallucinations.

                   JANOS
    Who? CIA?

                  ALEX (O.C.)
    MKUltra?

                    MAX
    Maybe. But...

    With some effort, Max reaches down
    beneath his chair.

                    MAX
    Got something for you.

Max pulls out a small REEL-TO-REEL
TAPE RECORDER with a built in speaker,
which he puts on the table and pushes
toward Janos

Janos's puzzled gaze goes from the tape
recorder to Max

                    MAX
        Go ahead.

Janos reaches over and CLICKS the play
button

The reels revolve. The tape HISSES. There is
the sound of a chair SCRAPING on a floor.

DISSOLVE TO:

INT. SOVIET PSYCHIATRIC UNIT - DAY

We see the same tape recorder on a
scuffed, plastic-topped table next to
an overflowing ASHTRAY and the PEAKED
UNIFORM HAT of an officer of the KGB.

Pulling away we see a white room, airy
and light with a window view of a snow
covered garden which is separated from
the dense forest beyond by a high,
chain linked fence.

A younger MAX dressed in a KGB uniform, sits at the table.

Opposite Max sits SERGEI in pyjamas and a dressing gown. His head has been shaved.

Max stubs out a cigarette.

Sergei strokes his bristly head. He looks intense, unblinking, but steady. Behind him by the door stands a meaty armed, soft-featured FEMALE ORDERLY.

> MAX
> You're looking good, Sergei.

> SERGEI
> I'm... lucid. Don't know for how long. It's an experimental treatment.

> MAX
> The Docs say you volunteered.

> SERGEI
> I've got a day, hours maybe. But I need to tell you. Warn you.

> MAX
> Warn me?

SERGEI

The KGB. The Soviet people. The
Revolution.

MAX

About what?

SERGEI

Maas. About Maas.

Max smirks but his eyes momentarily dart
downward. He scratches his nose.

MAX

Maas is nothing but a collection of
mask wearing weirdos and Eurotrash
dilettantes using a hedge fund to
PR up a fantasy that they run the
world. Trust me, they're not the
Illuminati, just a mediocre art
project. Albeit an expensive one.

SERGEI

I worked it out. It was a trap.

MAX

Well. Yes. But who? CIA? MI6?

SERGEI

Maas. Maas set the trap.

                    MAX

          Maas? Why?

                    SERGEI

          The Master.

                    MAX
                  (laughs)
          The skeleton key? A bunch of
          artsy-types take on the KGB for
          a trick key?

                    SERGEI

          To make a point. Don't you see?

Max lights a cigarette and flicks
the match in the ashtray on the table
between them. He shakes his head.
Sergei notices the MATCHBOX in Max's
hand. Quick as a striking snake Sergei
grabs Max's wrist.

Max tries to pull away but can't break
Sergei's grasp or his iron, intense
stare.

The Female Orderly takes a step forward.
She magics a LOADED SYRINGE out of
nowhere.

Max sees her, shakes his head. She takes
a step back.

                    SERGEI
        Let me see.

Max opens his hand. In it is a battered
matchbox labelled 'Pioneer'.

Sergei falls back in his chair. Laughs.

                    SERGEI
        Autosuggestion. Planting ideas,
        concepts, madness in our minds.
        In all of our minds. First, I thought
        it was from the moment we walked
        through the door of that place.
        The pictures. The lighting. The
        architecture, even. Visual cues.

                    MAX
        First?

                    SERGEI
        Who sent us chasing after a stash
        of looted paintings? Where did that
        notion come from? Does anyone know?

                    MAX
        This is a rabbit hole, Sergei.

                    SERGEI
          You know what I studied? Before
          I was recruited?

Max shakes his head.

                    SERGEI
          Reactionary and counter-revolutionary
          impulse in 19th Century French art.

                    Max
               (laughs, not unkindly)
          Well, it's good to know we had such
          a pro on our side.

                    SERGEI
          I'm not even sure how I ended up
          becoming a specialist in Degas.
          Or joining the KGB. Or even in
          Copenhagen. I mean, how many
          unmarried guys do you know get
          a foreign posting straight away?
          It seems almost predetermined.

                    MAX
          Hold up. You're saying Maas was
          setting you up - personally - for
          years? Just for this job?

                    SERGEI
Like a sleeper. A piece in a game.
To be called upon when required. A
gamble maybe.

                     MAX
Maas was in his 20s in 1975. You're
saying he somehow stage-managed your
career when he was what, a teenager?
A child? No one, nobody is that
smart, nothing is that powerful.

                    SERGEI
Maas is. Don't you see? He set this
up. Just to make a point. That's why
he took the Master keys. Made us go
mad. Disappeared in a puff of smoke.

                     MAX
Point?

                    SERGEI
You know that old proverb. When two
men meet, one must dominate.

Max stubs out his cigarette. He looks
tired and a little sad.

                     MAX
How long you got?

                         SERGEI
             What?

                          MAX
             How long before... You know.

Max points at his head, makes a 'mad'
face.

Sergei stares at Max. Leans forward.
There's a long silence.

                        SERGEI
                (nods to Max's cigarette)
             Gimme one of those things.

Max shakes a gasper free from a crumpled
pack. Sergei takes it. Max strikes a
match. Struggles to hold it still as
he lights Sergei's cigarette.

Sergei looks sat Max's shaking hand and
then into his old colleagues eyes. He
takes Max's hand and holds it steady
as he applies the match flame to his
cigarette.

                        SERGEI
             You know. Don't you?

                         MAX
        I know the medication you're on.
        When it stops working, then...

                        SERGEI
        I'm never coming back from Happy
        Land. Yeah. The doc was very clear.

                         MAX
        You volunteered anyway.

Sergei makes a 'yeah, but whatcha gonna
do?' shrug. Max flicks something from
his eye.

                        SERGEI
        Heh. Killed myself to bring you old
        news.

Max nods.

                         MAX
        Listen. Maas - they're no one.
        It's a ghost story at worst. At best,
        it's some kind of reactionary art
        installation designed by a bourgeois
        elite that cannot accept the
        inevitability of worker-led world
        revolution. It was Western agents
        that did for Borzoi and Uri. Yes?

Sergei searches Max's eyes. Looks down at his colleague's hand, sees the bourgeois affectation of a gold wedding band that Max plays with nervously.

> SERGEI
> Sure. Yes.

Max stands up, grateful. Takes his hat and places it on his head. He gives Sergei a salute.

Max returns a weary tap of his eyebrow.

> SERGEI
> Thanks for the cigarette.

Max nods, leaves, forgetting the tape recorder which continues to run.

Sergei leans back in his chair and takes a long, last drag, exhales. The smoke drifts upward, picked out in the SLATS OF SUN-LIGHT shining through the barred window.

DISSOLVE TO:

INT. MOSCOW FLAT - DAY

A huge BANG from a nearby RPG strike
shakes dust up in Max's flat. The motes
dance in the SLATS OF SUNLIGHT shining
through the blinds.

Older Max leans forward and switches off
the reel-to-reel tape recorder.

He leans back, icy cool. Examines Janos'
face.

                    MAX
          Lot of trouble for this story, boys.
          Lot of money.

Janos takes the hint, reaches into his
inside pocket and produces an ENVELOPE
STUFFED WITH $100 BILLS, drops it on
the table next to the tape recorder.

Max nods, but leaves the money where it
is, uncounted.

                    MAX
          Lot of trouble for a story you can't
          tell.

                    JANOS
          It'll be unattributed.

                         MAX
                   (laugh/cough)
          That hardly matters.

                         JANOS
          The KGB? They going to stop us?

                         MAX
          Look out the window, boys. We lost.
          Big Mac wrappers in Red Square by
          next year. KGB is already a relic.

                         JANOS
          What? Are you saying Maas is gonna
          stop us?
                   (laughs)
          They're good at keeping a secret.
          You're the first new source in
          two years. But you said it...

          Max pulls a 'said what?' Face.

                         JANOS
          You said it was a ghost story.
          They're not the Illuminati. Maas
          isn't the high priest of some
          new world order. It's just art.

                         MAX
          Art?

                    JANOS

          Not even that. Money. Marketing.
          Burnishing the Maas brand by
          making random events look
          orchestrated by them.

                    MAX

          That's what you think?

                    JANOS

          Sure. Trust me, if I dress this
          story up. Write it like a short
          work of fiction, say. It'll get
          published. It preserves the myth.
          If the Foundation exists, they
          should be happy with me.

     Max smiles. Leans forward. Picks up the
     wad of money. Considers it. Tucks it in
     his cardigan pocket.

                    MAX

          Yeah. Sure.

                    ALX (O.c.)

          So, what happened? To Sergei?

                    MAX

          To Sergei? Suicide. A day after this
          recording.

                          243

                    JANOS
          I can understand. But how? I'm
          guessing it was a secure unit.

                    MAX
          Very. Sergei was under constant
          watch, he was our only living
          lead. And yet.

Max leans forward, his voice lowers.

                    MAX
          His guard leaves his post for a
          minute. Grab a piss or something.
          Hears quiet footsteps in the
          corridor behind him, like a woman's.
          Turns. Nothing. Suddenly the lights
          go out. And Sergei starts shrieking
          from within his locked room. Then
          silence. Guard says it was the most
          terrible thing he'd ever heard.
          Shook him up, you know. And this guy
          fought halfway across Afghanistan.
          He forces himself to run back to
          Sergei's cell. Fumbles away with the
          key in the dark. Key won't turn in
          the lock. Guard realises... The door
          is unlocked. Swears he locked it
          himself. And yet it's open. He
          bursts inside, gun up. No light
          in the room. There's a motionless

                          244

shadow on the bed. Guard closes in.
It's Sergei. Dead... He'd strangled
himself to death with his own hands.

                    JANOS
Christ. Is that even possible?

                    MAX
The doc who examined him said
so. And who am I to argue with a
professional? I saw the corpse
myself. And, well, you could see
the hand marks around his neck,
so deep and fierce his windpipe
was near crushed flat.

                    ALEX (O.C.)
Shit.

                    MAX
Only thing is. Sergei had hands like
shovels. These handprints were much
smaller.
                    (beat)
Like those of a young girl.

Max leans back. Takes a huff of oxygen.
Smiles, cold and cruel.

Janos eyes skitter over Max's face.

                    JANOS
          Bullshit. You're shitting us.

Max is amused. Gives a shrug.

                    MAX
          I look forward to reading your story.

A huge nearby EXPLOSION rattles the
building and causes the lights to
flicker.

We see the POV of the camera as it drops
to the floor in a shower of plaster.

                  ALEX (O.C.)
          Fuck. That was close.

Alex (OC) picks up the camera. Adjusts
the focus to catch Max smirking.

Max flicks some plaster off his shoulder.

                    MAX
          You boys be careful now.

The camera remains on Max's smirking,
gaunt face, then cuts out with a sudden
HISS OF STATIC.

FADE OUT

In Silence

‐

'I knew how the story ended now, the only way it ever could, not with words, but…

…in silence.'

Burning embers fluttered down out of the ink-black clouds, fireflies in the night, the only illumination amidst the growing storm. I kept driving, kept moving forward, on and on through the desolate landscape, even though I couldn't see more than six feet in front of me. The headlights reached out like the trembling hands of a child in a dark room, disappearing into nothingness.

I had been driving for longer than I could remember. Running on empty for miles. The car would soon slow and stutter to a stop and, although I had no idea where I was, I knew I was far from home and further still from my destination. Night had fallen fast across this barren and empty land and with it, any hope of finding my way back to civilization.

My eyes burned with concentration and ached for sleep. I had started to see things that weren't there. Shapes in the night. Movements within the clouds of soot and ash that hung in the air. Patterns in the ancient, volcanic rock. I tried to focus on the small patch of visible road illuminated before me; the road, and the road alone. Everything else was a distraction.

After miles of featureless concrete and gravel, I saw a patch of light shimmer on the road, like ice or broken glass. I swerved to avoid it and felt the car tilt heavily to the right as the front wheel slipped into an unseen trench by the roadside. The whole car lurched forward and then up, as I fought to steady it, and I heard the boot pop open with a thump. I hit the brakes and got out hurriedly as the contents of the boot, sheet after sheet of paper, began to drift out into the night sky. The manuscript.

I grabbed at it, snatching whole pages from the air and clutching them to my body, chasing those I couldn't reach as they blew away from the road and into the field.

It was only when I stopped to catch my breath and turned back that I realised how far I had run. The car had vanished, consumed by the darkness.

A burning ember spiralled gracefully from the sky above me, inches from my face. It was still raining fire. I hadn't considered this weather to be strange until that moment. I remembered flames, a burning room, paper and pages, the click-clack of an old typewriter. It felt like a lifetime ago.

'A burning room, with the pages of the manuscript strewn around me like fallen leaves. A burning room, where the air shimmers, the walls blister and bubble, and the ceiling writhes like a living thing, a sea of black smoke.'

I reached out and caught one of the golden embers, holding it carefully between my finger and thumb, and realised that it wasn't ash. It was a small fragment of paper, blackened and charred, the edges fringed with a fiery red glow, the paper lined with spidery black inscriptions I didn't recognise.

The symbols meant nothing to me, but my mind wasn't what it once was. I knew that, if little else. Perhaps my own manuscript would give me the answers. I gazed down at the crumpled sheets in my arms and recognised for the first time that they were blank, every last one.

'The words seemed to be alive. I watched as the ink ran like tears, spilling off the edges of the paper as if it were trying to escape the words it had once formed, until the address was illegible and the note fell apart in my hands, until the tips of my fingers were stained black.'

In the distance, a pair of golden lights flickered through the fog. They lay in the opposite direction to where I had come from, away from my car, far from the road, from any hope of returning to where I had come from.

There was only one way left to go. The twin lights, like the eyes of some monstrous face, the face of God, awaited me on the horizon. I let the pages in my arms fall away as I began to walk in the direction of their glow.

The lights were coming from the windows of an imposing structure of stone and glass, a grand yet dilapidated hotel that I would have thought long abandoned, had it not been for the shimmering glow behind the glass. I climbed the steps to the entrance, pushed open the heavy door, and found myself in a lobby of dark red, faded gold, and burnished wood, the walls lined with rows of books.

Although it was quiet inside, save for the crackle of a fire and the muffled sounds of music from the bar, I noticed a few guests in and around the lobby; a barrel-chested, silver-haired man in his 60s in a chair by the fire, a woman with a bruised face sat alone at the bar, a mother and daughter, both dressed in black, like professional mourners, standing by the elevator. They each turned and looked at me casually, as you would at anyone passing before your line of sight. And yet, there was a trace of something in their eyes I didn't like, a pitying look, and a trace of recognition, as if they were trying to recall my face from a dream they had almost forgotten. There was something else too; something that made me feel as if they were not what they appeared to be at all; tired actors going through the motions in cliched roles, players on a hotel stage set recycled from a bad television movie.

'Every reader changes the story, bringing it to life
and making it real, every reader plays their part,
just as I have played mine.'

At the reception desk, a sallow-skinned man in a faded crimson uniform stood gazing at me with a sad smile and small, cruel eyes. I walked across the lobby towards him, passing over an intricately patterned, two-toned carpet, a maze without an exit. As I opened my mouth to speak, I realised that the song that was playing in the bar was an old favourite.

'I've been waiting for you,' I heard myself say.

'And you've been coming to me'" replied the man behind the desk.

'For such a long time now.'

'Yes... for such a long time now,' he said, echoing my words.

I smiled, overcome with a feeling of sorrow and regret; a realisation that I had lost something very important a long time ago and could never get it back.

'Do I need to sign anything?' I added after a moment.

On the counter lay a leather-bound guest book. The concierge, or was he the owner of this place, turned the ledger around and slid it across the desk towards me.

'You already have.'

I looked down at the words written in black ink. They had no meaning to me. In the distance, the woman at the bar began to laugh loudly. One by one the guests joined her until their laughter was all I could hear.

I thought I knew how the story ended.

I was wrong.

Nothing ever ends.

Nothing ever ends.

Acknowledgements

This collection is dedicated to Elliott, Evie, Etta, and Inga.

With special thanks to Christiane Domino for her generous patronage, heartfelt thanks to Zena and Colin Thomson, and to Inga Hillens for her constant support.

Thank you to everyone who contributed to this collection and made it possible, in particular book designer Peter Barnfather and publisher Jamie McGarry. Special thanks also to Maureen Hosay for the original idea for this book and to photographer Envela Castel for the cover image.

With additional thanks and acknowledgments to Professor Brian Ward, Professor Claire Nally, Bryan Talbot, Graeme Macrae Burnet, Paul Fulcher, Graham Fulcher, Jackie Law, Jonathan Pool, Jason Denness, Alison McCulloch, Michael Cullinane, Milka Ivanova, Robert Pisani, Mike Corrao, Samuel Moss, Andrew Wilt, Rick Schober, Alba Galmes, Sean Murphy, Ross Jeffery, Barbara Horne, Laura Barnard, Ben Lindner, Seth Corwin, Robert Pisani, Devyani Sen, Linda Hill, Liz Barnsley, Daniel Stubbings, Harry Whitewolf, Rachel Louise Atkin, Andrew Mitchell, Trevor Pill, Peter Whitfield, Dean Forbes, Vicky Blacklock, Shirley Morgan, Iain Smith, Tom Abba, Marcus Pactor, Matt Lombardi, David Hepworth, Sue Harrison, Clare Pepper, Dave Dawe, Sophie O'Neill, Ciaran O'Melia, Richard Barnett, Ella Holder, Rebecca Gray, Heimo Vuorinen, and Sam Molloy.

Contributors

Dr Daniel Barnes-Bineid is a London-based writer, editor, and teacher. He has published articles and reviews in *Aesthetica*, *FAD Magazine*, *this is tomorrow*, *ArtSlant*, and more. His book, *The Value Industry: Reflections on Art, Money and Celebrity*, was published in 2019.

P M Buchan has written for publications including *Times Literary Supplement*, *Starburst* and *SCREAM: The Horror Magazine*, and his transgressive work has been featured in *Rue Morgue*, *Kerrang*, and *Fortean Times*. He loves horror-punk and the Romantics. pmbuchan.com / pmbuchan.substack.com.

Matthew Cook is the author of the novel *Life on Other Planets* (Lendal Press, 2020). His short story 'Thresholds' was shortlisted for the 2020 Cambridge Short Story Prize, and his other work has appeared in *The Stockholm Review*, *Oblong Magazine*, *Number Eleven*, *Imbroglio*, and the Cool Dog Short Story Prize, among others. He works as a freelance writer and lives in Liverpool.

Ted Curtis is a writer working in all fields, except advertising. During the 1990s, he had success as a writer, even with Serpent's Tail, but decided to concentrate on his drinking. He was very good at it too. Now's he back and working on new writing. His novel, *The Darkening Light*, was published in 2014. New work can be viewed at: antsy-pantsy.blogspot.com.

Hanna ten Doornkaat is a German-born artist who is based in the UK and holds an MA Sculpture from the Wimbledon School of Art. Her work has been exhibited widely to critical acclaim and is held in collections internationally.

Associate Professor Mike Jeffries is an ecologist based in Newcastle, who has a particular fondness for lo-fi DIY culture, collage, cuts-ups, and zines.

Dr Magdalena Harper is a photographer and freelance writer. Her body of work includes short stories, film scripts, novels, theatre pieces, and collage poetry. She self-published her debut novel *Midnight Motel* in 2020.

Maureen Hosay is a PhD student in Children's Literature at the University of Antwerp Belgium. Other interests include experimental literature (she wrote her MA thesis on Mark Z. Danielewski's *House of Leaves*), detective stories, and surrealism.

Dr Helen Gørrill is an artist, author, and editor in the arts, with a research interest in gendered transnational aesthetics. Gorrill's practice is prolific and diverse, stemming from international artist residencies – and she is one of the few British artists (alongside Tracey Emin) to have her work selected for New York Brooklyn Museum's digital EASCFA archive. She is currently in a three-book deal with Bloomsbury Academic Press (London & New York): firstly, *Women Can't Paint: Gender, the Glass Ceiling and Values in Contemporary Art* (2020); secondly, her new upcoming monograph for Bloomsbury, *War Paint: Gender Inequality in the Virtual Artworld*; and thirdly, the upcoming *Wife, Witch, Whore: Essential Conversations about Gender, Art and Culture*.

Amy Lord is a writer from North-East England. Her debut novel, *The Disappeared*, was published by Unbound in 2019. She won a Northern Writers' Award in 2015 for *The Disappeared* and was also longlisted in the inaugural Bath Novel Award. Amy is currently working on a new novel. She also writes short stories and flash fiction and has had work published by *Reflex Fiction*, *The London Reader* and *Palm-Sized Press*.

Marc Nash is an author/fictioneer of 11 books and his twelfth *The Death of The Author (In Triplicate)* deals with many of the themes in this essay. His novel *Three Dreams In The Key Of G* was shortlisted for the 2018 Not The Booker Prize.

John Palmer is a writer of predominantly transgressive fiction and is working on his first novel. He is the editor of *Cult Fiction*, a website and ongoing project to share his passion for literature and creative writing. The website link is: cultfiction.co.uk.

Meaghan Ralph is an artist from the Hamptons and a known liar. She worked with Warhol at The Factory and knew Ezra Maas before he was famous. She enjoys knitting, hot yoga, and conversing with llamas, MR is currently working on her first book.

Nick Reeves (aka Henry Eves) combs beaches, cuts hair & counts magpies (latest tally 10). He has been published by *Experiments in Fiction*, *Gleam Magazine*, and *Free Verse Revolution*. His fiction and poetry can be found at nickreeves.blog.

Ian Roden lives on the border between Gateshead and County Durham where he writes and rides horses. *The Master* was his first foray into post-modernist translation. He is currently working on a number of screenplays for film and television companies.

Further Reading

Abel, C. *Hybrid Ontologies*. University of Harvard Press, Boston, MS, 2004 (720-3116-4964-01).

Adley, J. *Architectures of Credibility*. University of Weyland, AU, 2001 (711 4689-32109-1).

Agrippa, H. *Three Books of Occult Philosophy*. Theophania Publishing, 1533 (177-083040-5).

Althusser, L. *Ideology and Ideological State Apparatus: On The Reproduction of Capitalism*. Verso Books, 1968 (978-1781681640).

Andelic, P. *Radical Ecologies in Contemporary US Art History*. Yale With A Six Press, 1999 (1791492003182).

Archer, M. *Art Since 1960*. Thames & Hudson, 1997 (0-500-20298-2).

Atkin, R.L. *Less Than Zero: Maas Consumerism in the Brat Pack Generation*. Sheffield Steel Books, 1998 (0-349-90421-1).

Atkins, TJ. *Critical Maas: A Life in Art*. Bloomsbury, 1987 (978-21298-21-3).

Auge, M. *Non-Places: Introduction to an Anthropology of Supermodernity*. Verso, 1992 (8601404397103).

Baillie-Smith, A. *Z is for Zurich: Maas in Switzerland*. Winter Hill Books, 1994 (2-5693-911245-1).

Bantum, I. *Masterpiece: How One Artist Fooled The World*. Cook and Co Press, 1990 (0-15-0145615-4).

Barnes, M. *Elblondino in the West*. Cucumber Press, 1991 (978-00031-911).

Barnsley, L. *New Perspectives: Post-War Artists*. Oxford Books, 1995 (98-11134-72391-1).

Barnard, L. *Topology of the Mind: An Illustrated Guide.* Peterborough Press, 2001 (2-679-012311-1).

Barrow-Wearmouth, H. *The Road to Hell: Ergodic Art and Intermedia Performance.* Johnston Press, 1999 (9-14529-3881-1).

Beauvais, A. *Exposing the Truth: Power and Propaganda in the Age of Fake News.* Le Monde Books, 2010 (0-75901-23941-1).

Beauvoir, S. *The Ethics of Ambiguity.* Open Road Media, 1947 (978-1504054225).

Berger, J. *Ways of Seeing.* Penguin Books, 1972 (0-14-013515-4).

Blacklock, V, *Apples and Black Coffee: An Artist's Life.* Ellison Books, 2011 (3-62901-42971-3).

Bogain, A. *Rum, Rum, Rum: Maas Under The Influence.* St Germain Books, France, 2001 (873-4529-1552-9).

Bogenschneider, JL. *New Fictions: Intersections in 20th Century Art and Contemporary Literature.* Eden Press, 2001 (978-1312453266).

Boyle, T. *Artistic Horizons.* Devil Dinosaur Books, 2010 (978-15040542).

Brownlee, L. *Mining the Past: Archaeologies of Knowledge.* Durham Press, 1997 (454-01129-989-12).

Buchan, P. *The Heart of Things.* Bleach Books, 2001 (978-45431-981).

Camus, A. *The Myth of Sisyphus.* Vintage International, 1942 (978-0141023991).

Cann, H. *Mapping Reality.* Moon Palace Books, 2004 (399-08791-5650-2).

Castel, E. *The Image Tells Me Death In the Present: Maas and Photographic Art.* Dionysus Books, 1991 (787-0194-404-1).

Carroll, S. *Something Deeply Hidden.* Elcot Press, 1985 (9-014921-041).

Chambers, R. *The King in Yellow*. F. Tennyson Neely, 1895 (978-1840226447).

Cook, M. *Totality of Informational Objects*. FME Books, 1996 (7010-00344-0-111).

Collins, J. *Hardboiled Art*. Neo-Noir Press, New Zealand, 1995 (00110-4330-1001).

Corrao, M. *Exploring the Gutter: Marginal Spaces in Art and Literature*. Smut-Maker Press, 2010 (1-92239-4664-21).

Cornis-Pope, M. *New Literary Hybrids in the Age of Multimedia Expression*. John Benjamins Publishing, Amsterdam, 2014 (978-90-272-3463-6).

Cozell, K. *Memories of the Future: Apocalypse Now?* Whitfield Books, 2020 (ISBN 6-90101-345-971).

Cullinane, M. *The Dryer Will Change Your Life*. University of New Cork, 2008 (0-198234-89-11).

Curtis, T. *Continuous Spectra*. Old London Books, 1991 (1-095134-98234).

Crowley, A. *The Book of Lies*. Frater Perdurabo, 1912 (1-0877285160).

Debord, G. *Society of the Spectacle*. Zone Books, 1967 (0-942299-79-5).

Denness, J. *Late 20th Century Gnomological Art*. F is Fake Press, 1999 (0-770885206).

Derrida, J. *Glas*. University of Nebraska Press, 1985 (0-8032-6581-6).

Deleuze, G. & Guattari, F. *A Thousand Plateaus*. Les Éditions de Minuit, 1980 (978-0816614028).

Elliott, K. *A Grammatology of Psychoanalysis in Late 20th Century Art*. Ryton Books, 2010 (978-0803265813).

Fawcett, R. *Video Art and Hidden Signs: Transmitting the Real*. BFM Books, 2003 (978-0803265813).

Fallowell, D. *20th Century Characters*. Vintage, London, 1994 (978-0803265813).

Feynman, R. *The Feynman Lectures on Physics, Vol. 1: Mainly Mechanics, Radiation, and Heat*. Addison Wesley, 1963 (978-0-1-34519-0).

Fisher, Mark. *Late Capitalism: Is There Any Alternative?* Zero Point Books, UK, 2011 (978-1-84694-317-1).

Forbes, D.A. *Maas Hysteria: A History of Conspiracies*. DSBF Press, 1998 (978-1-14392-535-1).

Forbes, D.A. *Pynchon Myself: The Untold Story*. Brother Books, 2001 (978-1-05293-711-3).

Foucault, M. *Death and the Labyrinth*. Doubleday and Co Inc, London, 1986 (0-8264-6435-1).

Foucault, M. *Madness and Civilisation: A History of Madness in the Age of Reason*. Random House, New York, 1965 (978-0415255394).

Fulcher, G. & Fulcher, P. *Twin Psychologies and Fatal Symmetries*. Oxford University Press, 2000 (978-1-44691-412-3).

Furno, J. & N. *Electronic Art and Modes of Production*. Hepscott Books, 1989 (978-1-94493-116-5).

Galmes, A. *Maas in Spain: A Comprehensive Art History*. Island Press, 1991 (978-1-34654-110-7).

George, N. *Temporal Lows: Depression and Time in the work of Ezra Maas*. Zero Sum Books, 2005 (978-0803265813).

Glass, D. *Into Infinity: Maas and the Impossible*. 20th Century Books, London, 1993 (978-0803265813).

Gørrill, H. *Women Can't Paint*. Bloomsbury Books, 2020 (9781501352768).

Green, C. *The Third Hand: Collaboration in Art from Conceptualism to Postmodernism*. University of Minnesota Press, 2001 (978-0816637133).

Green, M. *Ghosts of Maas: Research as Creative Practice / Practice as Research in 20th Century Art & Literature*. Antigone Press, 1999 (978-0803265813).

Gray, A. *Lanark*. Canongate Books, 1981 (978-1782117148).

Hausmann, R. *Following the Maaster*. Cambridge Press, 2008 (9781001452411).

Heidegger, M. *Being and Time*. SUNY Press, 1927 (978-1438432762).

Hepworth, D. *The Endless Library*. Tyne Bridge Publishing, 2008 (720-3116-4964).

Hill, L. *Antinomies of the Real*. Routledge, 1994 (978-1113265813).

Hodgson, P. *What's Happening, Dude? Art in the 1960s*. Stripes El Hodeo Press, 1996 (978-6713165211).

Horne, B. *Forgeries and Replicas: The Art of Reproduction*. Printed Word Books, 2001 (978-383122544).

Hosay, M. *Letters from M: Lost Correspondence*. Francophile Books, 2002 (978-0803265813).

Hossenfeld, S. *Lost in Math*. Hachette, 2020 (978-1541646766).

Hopesmith, S. *A Poetics of Sin: Studies of Negative Space in Post-War Art*. Elspeth Books, 2020 (978-0803265813).

Hughes, R. *The Shock of the New: Art and the Century of Change*, Thames & Hudson, 1980 (0-500-27582-3).

Hutton, J. *Aporias: A Retrospective*. Newbridge Books, 2001 (9-1844657477).

Ivanova, M. Rhizome: *Secret Interactions & Hidden Meanings: The Intersection of Media and Communications with Literature and Art: 1950 to the present*. Liberia Press, 1998 (720-3116-4964-01).

James, Daniel. *The Unauthorised Biography of Ezra Maas*. 1st Edition, Dead Ink Books, 2018, (9781911585299).

James, Daniel. *The Unauthorised Biography of Ezra Maas*. New and Expanded Edition, Valley Press, 2022 (978-0913213-2).

Jameson, Fredric. *The Detections of Totality*. Verso Books, 2016 (978-1-78478-216-0).

Janes, I. *Politics, Poetics, Culture, and Jack Daniel's*. Hancock Press, 2001 (720-1065-1164-3).

Jeffries, M. *The Geography of Art as Investigative Anthropology*. Zine Press, 1999 (720-0116-1222-1).

Jeffrey, R. *The Last Beat*. Tome Books, 1995 (978-2051-2994-1).

Kaku, M. *Physics of the Future*. DoubleDay Books, 2011 (978-0-385-53080-4).

Karabekian, R. *Be Careful What We Pretend To Be: The Art of Performance*. Bluebeard Books, 1979 (978-1001-3511-1).

Kelly, M. *Unknown Country: Historical Mysteries in Contemporary Art*. Bridge Press, 1999 (720-022-4554-01).

Kendal, R. *The Meditative Relationship between Modern Art and Cycling*. Bay City Books, 2002 (978-113-54579-1).

Kenner, E. *H.W Maas: The Tangier Letters – 1945–1965*. Routledge, 1980 (978-019034-1).

Khan, H. *Proto-conceptual Art: Maas, the Japan Years*. JR Books, 2002 (978-2-45472-3).

King, V. *Coffee and Apples: A Writer's Life*, Ellison Books, 2011 (0-393-00079-6).

King, D. *The Commissar Vanishes: The Falsification of Art and Photographs in Stalin's Russia*. Canongate, 1997 (978-0-86241-724-6).

Koolman, H. *New Perspectives on Contemporary Art*. Kingston Books, 2007 (978-12065-342-1).

Lacan, J. *The Four Fundamental Concepts of Psychoanalysis*. W.W Norton Books, 1974 (0-393-00079-6).

Lacey, M. *A Short History of Tall Collage Arts.* Ambient Media, 2009 (978-3-65611-5).

Law, J. *Methodological Rationale for the Taxonomy of Post-War Conceptual Art.* Queen Books, 1995 (978-393-2547-1).

LeVay, A. *The Satanic Bible.* Avon Books, 1969 (0-393-00079-6).

Linde, A. *Particle Physics and Inflationary Cosmology.* CRC Books, 1990 (978-3718604906).

Loeb, C. *The Follower and The Following: A Tangled History of Cults and Conspiracies.* Third Eye Books, 1999 (978-23761-98-0).

Lopez, B. *International Literary Review: Post-War Artists.* University of Madrid, 2000 (978-04571-989-0).

Lowes, R. *Woman in Black: A Study of Helena Maas.* Brunel Books, 1998 (978-23311-545-0).

Lusted, K. *Eastern Influences.* New Tokyo Press, 1999 (978-1504054225).

Maas, H.E. *Ezra Maas: A Life in Art – Collected Letters.* Maas Foundation Publishing, 2005 (978-54890I-879-0).

MacIntyre, G. *A Life In Journalism: From Barstools to Broadsheets.* Beehive Books, 2004 (978-15398-012-1).

McCulloch, A. *Maas Education: The Artist's Early Years.* Oxford Comma Press, 1995 (978-88910-98-0).

McHale, Brian. *Postmodern Fiction.* Methuen, 1987 (0-416-36400-4).

McGee, S. *There's Someone In Your House.* RBS Books, 1983 (978-567321-0).

Mitchell, A. *Who Shot The Sheriff?* Dunston Press, 1991 (978-29-030393-1).

Molloy, S. *Truth in The Age of Insanity.* Soho Square Books, 2019 (978-81923-011).

Moreno Esparza, G. *Translations: New Studies in 21st Century Journalism*. Versus Press, 2014 (978-13392-834-1).

Morgan, S. *Death in the work of 20th Century Artists (Oh, Great Extinctor)*. Boots & Co Books, 2001 (978-01199-23-1).

Morris, E. *Conversations on Trains*. Manor Books, 1997 (720-3116-4964-01).

Moss, S. *The Method of Totality*. Van Life Media, 2011 (978-01199-23-1).

Moss, S. *Land Art, Sound, Literature – An Odyssey Across America*. Van Life Media, 2009 (978-01199-23-1).

Murray, L. *Salt Lake City, Baby*. Murritski Press, 1999 (978-01199-23-1).

Murphy, A. *Forest of Signs and Symbols*. University of Maynard, 1998 (978-34301-00).

Nally, C. *The Centre Cannot Hold: Death, Art, Literature, Goth Culture*. Black Cat Books, 2003 (978-45431-981).

Napier, J. *The Squared Circle*. Wildcard Books, 2001 (978-45431-981).

Nash, M. *Which World Is This?* New Realities Press, 1998 (978-45431-981).

O'Neill, P. *The Comedy of Entropy*. Toronto University Press, 1990 (0-8020-2737-7).

Page, H. *A Specified Egg: The Liverpool Art Scene*, HP Press, 2001 (978-454032-01).

Palmer, JA. *Cult Fiction: An Unauthorised Bible*. Black Tee Books, 1989 (978-45431-981).

Parr, C. *Sound and Fury – The Trouble with Ezra Maas*, NI Publishing, 2004 (978-333401-01).

Pisani, R. *Island Living: The Artist as Island*. Maltese Falcon Press, 2009 (978-97524-89-1).

Pill, T. *A Design For Life*. Cramlington Place Books, 2011 (720-3116-4964-01).

Pool, J. *An Infinite Sphere*, University of Cambridge Press, 1998 (978-90221-34-1).

Ralph, M. *You're the Boss, Applesauce*. Yaphank Press, Long Island, New York, 2001 (978-34511-091).

Reeves, N. *Falling for Philosophers*. Van Gogh Books, Amsterdam, 1991 (978-45431-990).

Reeves, N. *Berlin, Bowie, and Ezra Maas: 1977–1979*. Van Gogh Books, Amsterdam, 1991 (720-3116-4964-01).

Rhizome, J. *Don't Watch The Film: A Warning*. Cult Press, 2001 (978-31190-881).

Ring, P. *Epistemological Architecture*. NU Press, 2001 (978-228190-09).

Roden, I. *Make Your Own Freedom*. Epitome Press, 1994 (978-22301-44-1).

Rovelli, C. *Reality Is Not What It Seems*. Penguin Books, 2017 (978-0141983219).

Rudd, A. *The Girl from Gateshead*. Malbec Press, 1979 (978-79901-64-01).

Sartre, J. *Existential Is A Humanism*. Yale University Press, 1946 (978-0300115468).

Schober, R. *The World Needs Tough Poets Too*. Boston Books, 1985 (978-43109-01).

Schlesinger, P. H. *Maas and Memory: The Proliferation of False Memories in Late 20th Century and Early 20th Century Culture*. Goldman Books, 2011 (978-56113-001).

Schlain, L. *Art and Physics, Parallel Visions in Space, Time, and Light*. Perennial Press, HarperCollins, 1991 (0-688-12305-8).

Sen, D. *Pandemonium: Art and Chaos*. New Delhi Press, 1989 (720-3116-4964-01).

Sheldon, N. *The Happening: New York Art from 1964–1969*. Banana Bread Books, 1981 (941-1-08342-879).

Sheridan, A. *The Order of Things: An Archaeology of the Human Sciences*. Vintage Books, 1973 (978-1-85984-421-2).

Slowey, A. *Art in the Age of Aquarius*. Wet Bandit Books, 1995 (720-3116-4964-01).

Smith, A. *Performing Performance Art*. Brown & Co, 1985 (454-1-0232965-2).

Stefanos, Kim. *A History of Religious Esoterica*. Third Eye Books, London, 1979 (978-0-97801-23989).

Stephens, R. *American Dreamer*. Kansas City Press, 1999 (978-05981-433-2).

Stubbins, D. *Between the Dimensions: Ezra Maas in the Seventies*. Victory Books, 2001 (720-3116-4964-01).

Stuckrad, K. *Western Esotericism, A History of Secret Knowledge*. Routledge Press, 2005 (9-1844657477).

Summerfield, J. *Maas and Mixology*. Poison Cabinet Books, BX, 2000 (978-1-25214-555-2).

Surtees, G. *Black and White: Perspectives on the Art Industry*. Kendal Press, 1991 (9-1844657477).

Squire, H. *Truth and Perception: Conversations on Journalism and Art*. York Media, 1985 (978-1-75183-545-2).

Taylor, C. *Maas on Film*. Jam Jar Press, 1991 (978-1-33934-515-2).

Teleaga, A. *Photographic Studies*. Silver Press, 1979 (978-1-15981-00-1).

Thomson, C. & Z. *New Artistic Origins*. St Peters Press, 1985 (978-1-35934-224-2).

Thomson, G. *The Literature of Class Aesthetics*. Lockhart Books, 2005 (978-6-25654-221-2).

Turner, R. *Who was Adrian Nash? Lost Artist Series*. RF Books, 2004 (9-1844657477).

Vale, J. *Transference, Art in New York: 1965–1985*. Getty Books, 1998 (978-1-25914-525-2).

Van-Hensbergen, C. *A Brief History of Postmodern Art.* Jesmond House Press, 1991 (978-1-25682-320-2).

Various (Edited by Anonymous), *Collected Essays on The Unauthorised Biography of Ezra Maas.* Inside the Labyrinth Books, 2021 (978-02341-454-0).

Versluis, A. *Western Esoteric Traditions.* Versluis Books, 2007 (9780742558366).

Wallas, G. *Maas and the BBC: Interviews 1969–1979.* British Broadcasting Corporation Books, 2002 (978-1-15585-333-2).

Walker, J. *The United States of Paranoia: A Conspiracy Theory.* Harper Collins, 2013 (0062135554).

Ward, B. *Devil at the Crossroads: The King of the Delta Blues and the King of Contemporary Art.* Jumping Jack Books, 2003 (978-5-45681-523-3).

Watson, T. *Cult Horror Narratives: Maas and Absence.* Chainsaw Press, New York, 2001 (978-4-15980-121-3).

Watson, V. *Literary Voices in New Visual Art.* Di Meo Books, 2001 (978-0-15924-551-7).

Waugh, A. *Ghost Biographies.* Birdseye Books, 2001 (978-23144-00-1).

Webber, J. *The Great One: Ezra Maas.* Zeitgeist Press, 2006 (978-45331-99-2).

Whetstone, D. *Whatever Happened to Ezra Maas?* Culture Mag Press, 2004 (978-3-45581-221-5).

Whitewolf, H. *Albion! Albion! Maas and British Myth.* Lone Wolf Books, Brighton, 2009 (978-4-90134-461-3).

Whitfield, P. *Epistemological Continuities in Dead Time.* Fowles Books, 2012 (978-2-15963-711).

Willis, N. *Death and Illustration.* Mortuary Press, 1999 (978-03121-13-0).

Williams, T. *Walking the Dog: Maas and Meditation.* Ellison Press, 1998 (978-0-14951-701).

Wilt, A. *The Time Is...?* 11:11 Press, Minnesota, 2018 (978-3-759032-622-5).

Woolf, V. *Orlando.* Hogarth Press, 1928 (978-1-853262395).

Yau, J. *In the Realm of Appearances.* Hopewell, NJ, Ecco Press, 1993 (0-88001-298-6).

Wojtas, O. *An Education in Art: 1950 to the Present.* Samovar Books, 1995 (978-3-41174-543-0).

Zimmer, A. *A History of Underground and Cult Cinema: 1958–1999.* LA Skylight Books, 2004 (978-03275-221-1).

Žižek, S. *Welcome to the Desert of the Real.* Verso Books, 2002 (978-1-85984-421-2).

External link: ezramaas.com

The Unauthorised Biography of Ezra Maas

Daniel James

Ezra Maas is dead. The famously reclusive artist vanished without a trace seven years ago while working on his final masterpiece, but his body was never found. While the Maas Foundation prepares to announce his death, journalist Daniel James finds himself hired to write the untold story of the artist's life – but this is no ordinary book. The deeper James delves into the myth of Ezra Maas, the more he is drawn into a nightmarish world of fractured identities and sinister doubles.

A chilling literary labyrinth, *The Unauthorised Biography of Ezra Maas* blends postmodern noir with biography, newspaper clippings, artworks, photographs, letters, official documents, phone transcripts, emails, and handwritten notes, to create a book like no other before it.

This landmark, definitive edition of the novel features new material from the author and stunning visual content from an international group of artists, including Hanna Ten Doornkaat, Mike Corrao, Laura Barnard, Nick Loaring, The Printed Word, Ella Holder and Tiny Golden Books.

At the request of the author, £1 from every copy of this book sold will go to U.K. charity, Mermaids – supporting transgender, nonbinary and gender-diverse children, young people, and their families.